Blood on the Bluebonnets

Blood on the Bluebonnets

BILL LEHMANN

ISBN-13: 978-1519393517

ISBN-10: 1519393512

BLOOD
on the
Bluebonnets

A family History of the Miller, Lott, Lynch, Cohron, Wallace, Aikman, Posey and Lehmann settlers in early Texas from Austin's Colony to 1904.

They shed thier blood on the Bluebonnets

Andrew Miller, John Lott and Robert T. Miller were killed by Indians in early Texas. Matt Wallace was lynched by the Bill Posey gang at Waco, Texas in 1873. This event shattered the lives of te families and a change in their lives forever.

By Bill Lehmann

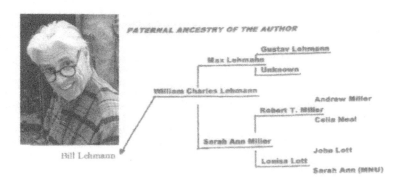

PATERNAL ANCESTRY OF THE AUTHOR

Bill Lehmann

William Charles Lehmann

Max Lehmann
Gustav Lehmann
Unknown

Sarah Ann Miller

Robert T. Miller
Andrew Miller
Celia Neal

Louisa Lott
John Lott
Sarah Ann (MNU)

FOREWORD

The Brazos River Valley of Texas was once a peaceful and serene paradise. Its great expanse was carpeted with native wildflowers and succulent grasses. Wildlife abounded. Its stillness was interrupted only occasionally by the shrieks of the Indian on buffalo hunting forays.

The area was inhabited by the Waco (Huecho) tribe of Indians, a Caddoan culture, who had chosen the clear waters of the Brazos River and its Tehuacana Creek tributaries for their settlements. After acquiring the Spanish horses that made them mobile, the Comanche and Kiowa Plains Indian tribes established the Comanche Trace, and regularly traversed this land as one of their favorite hunting grounds. The Wacos and the Plains tribes existed in a cautiously peaceful posture, and established a somewhat friendly trading relationship. White settlers seeking new lands and opportunity would change the scene forever. The American colonists had begun a steady push of migration south and west off the original colonies in Virginia and the Carolinas. Crossing the Appalachian Mountains, they had entered and settled new lands they called Georgia, Alabama, Tennessee, Florida and Mississippi. The westward expansion was accelerated with the Louisiana Purchase. Following the victory by the United States in 1814 against the British in the Louisiana bayous, the settlers had reached the mighty Mississippi River. There would be no turning back the tide of civilization. In fact, the cry for further expansion westward was reaching a thunderous roar that could be heard all the way to Washington. Joining this tumultuous movement west was the family of Andrew Miller, who settled first in Louisiana then came to Texas in 1824 as a member of Stephen F. Austin's colony. Miller secured his League of land (4,428 acres) from the Mexican government on Doe Run Creek, a tributary to the Brazos River. Following soon after were the families of John Lott, from Mississippi, via Florida; Benjamin Franklin Posey, from Alabama, and Washington S. Wallace, from North Carolina.

Fate would bring the Miller and Lott families together in Austin's colony, where they would carve out a new homestead in the wild frontier. There they would fight Indians, Mexicans and a hostile environment in trying to build their new homes and the dreams that were a part of the American family process.

As the frontier expanded, the Miller and Lott children would move north along the Brazos to the Tehuacana Valley, near present Waco, Texas. There they would still be beset with Indian problems; an always-terrible economy, and the hostile Texas weather that seemed to be in constant flood or drought. The Civil War was devastating to these families, as it was to the entire South.

Following the Civil War, an economic change showed great promise to the families in furnishing Texas beef to the Northern markets. The Tehuacana valley would now resound to the thundering hoof-beats of thousands of horses and cattle and the wild shouts of the cowboy moving cattle through the Waco area to the Chisholm Trail that ended in faraway Kansas. .

Cattle rustling, outlawry, the murder of a deputy sheriff, and the lynching of one of the family members before his anguished, pregnant wife would destroy their dreams of building a successful ranching operation. The turbulent times and events would split apart the families and change their lives forever.

The events would also create an outlaw whose name would strike fear in the lives of central Texas settlers, and who would meet his end in a violent blaze of gunfire in a new frontier called Indian Territory.

This is the story of these families who shed their blood on the Bluebonnets.

DEDICATION

Most people are curious about their family roots at one time or another. Since most of the Lehmann side of my family were either dead, or lived in Texas where I was not able to visit with them, I became even more curious as to the family tree.

I was only five years old when my father, Will Lehmann died. My mother knew very little about the Lehmann side but could go back several generations on her (the Warren) side. In later years I was able to visit with an uncle, Max Lehmann, a brother of my father, who lived most of his life in Garland, Texas. He was able to furnish only scant information about the family, and as I discovered later, much of it was erroneous. Sadly, I found most of my Texas relatives knew little, if anything, about their own parents, much less their ancestors. Death certificates, when they could be obtained, in most cases were unreliable because the knowledge of the family was practically non-existent by the children of the deceased.

Uncle Max was able to tell me his mother's maiden name was Sarah Miller, which turned out to be correct. He did not know who her mother and father were. Sarah had died in 1900 from appendicitis when all the Lehmann children were very small. Mexicans near San Antonio reportedly killed the father, Max Lehmann, in 1904 leaving the Lehmann children orphans. A sister, Louisa Augusta Lehmann, had married Tack Halliburton in 1901, and they had moved to Gonzales County and began married life on his father's ranch. Louisa and Tack raised the youngest Lehmann children until they were old enough to begin a life on their own.

In 1986, a search for family roots began. Rosemary and I went to the Oklahoma Historical Society in Oklahoma City where we began our search for family roots in Texas. Uncle Max had told me his father, Max Lehmann, was raised at Indianola, so our search began with the Calhoun County census in 1860. I looked at every name on the census rolls for the county, and was about to give up when I noticed the name Max and Paul on the census rolls as children of "Gustoff Laman." The census taker had spelled the names phonetically. I went to the 1870 census. They were still there in Indianola, and the name was beginning to be spelled more like the German spelling: It was now "Lehman"--somewhat better. There was no question but what this was the family we were seeking. The Lehmann mystery had been partially solved, now we could begin filling in the blanks.

The Miller side remained a mystery. It was not even known what county in Texas they may have lived, or who the mother and father of "Sarah Miller" could have been. We did know that Sarah had been married first to a man named Wallace, and two children had been born to the marriage...Sarah Emmaline and Matthew Alexander. We also knew her first husband, given name unknown, had lost his life by hanging, reportedly by rustlers he had surprised in the act of stealing livestock on their ranch. We also knew that after Sarah had married Max Lehmann, their first born was named Celia Frances, after Sarah's sister. Not much to go on, but the search must begin somewhere if we were to ever find out anything.

Rosemary and I began a search of Bell County, Texas, and branched off from there to adjoining counties where we searched every name on the census rolls looking for a Miller family. Several counties had been searched and we had spent many days at the Historical Society when a break finally came. I had found a Robert T. Miller family in Limestone County in the 1850 census. Robert T. Miller's wife was named Louisa and they had a daughter, "Cela" who was only a few months old in the census. The "Cela" could possibly be Celia, we thought, but all hopes were dashed when we were unable to find the family in the subsequent 1860 census. If this was "our" family the 1860 census would show my grandmother Sarah, for she was born in 1852, and would be shown on the 1860 census rolls.

In researching the 1860 census, family-by-family, Rosemary noticed a family named "Cohron" with several children, but listed at the bottom were "C.F. and Sarah Miller." Their personal property value was listed as fifteen hundred dollars each. The mother's name was Louisa! Could this be the family we were searching for? We thought it was a good possibility, but this was not to be determined until much later.

The Cohron family was listed in the Mt. Calm area of Limestone County. Also found in that census was a Wallace family of six children. One was a male child named M.A. Could this be the Wallace Sarah was first married to? The discovery had possibilities, but it would have to be put on hold until more extensive research could be devoted to the search for family roots.

In 1992, our son, Gene Lehmann, moved to Athens, Texas, where he assumed the editor's position at the Athens Daily Review. I felt this was an opportunity to continue the search, as it would afford personal examination of documents and other records that could be found only in the courthouse records. Beginning the research, I was able to find in libraries, courthouse records and other sources, the missing pieces of a puzzle I still am unable to believe has been put together.

It has been a fun and rewarding project. I have discovered new, interesting family members, and made friends with many new acquaintances. It has also given our family knowledge that our ancestors were among the first settlers in Texas, coming in with Stephen F. Austin's colony. Somewhat surprisingly, it was discovered most of our male ancestors died violent deaths from Indians, Mexicans and even their own family members. Hardly a death by natural causes can be attributed to any male family member until after 1904.

The information has been fascinating. Each new lead was followed with further search and revelation. It has been a real challenge to make these discoveries. It would not have been possible without the help of Rosemary, who spent countless hours looking at every name on the census rolls of several Texas counties, and then being able to spot the names of C.F. and Sarah Miller with another family because their father had died, and the mother, Louisa, had remarried. The fifteen hundred dollar personal property value owned by Celia and Sarah was the value of slaves left them by their father's estate. Another surprise!

This effort is therefore dedicated to Rosemary, who has made it possible.

THANKS TO SOME SPECIAL FOLKS

This family history could not have been accomplished without the help of many others. To obtain information on my family roots, of which I knew practically nothing, I have relied on books, newspapers, county and state records, census records, and interviews with interesting new acquaintances I made along the way in this two year search.

I am not a historian, and make no pretenses as such. I have borrowed liberally from books on the county and state history of Texas; the history of the Creek Nation and the history of Indian Territory, and tried to illustrate how the families would have fitted into the events of their times. This has been more than the work of one individual, and I would especially like to thank:

*The Texas State Library and Archives, Austin, Texas. What a magnificent collection of historical artifacts. Thanks to Donaly E. Brice, and the helpful staff.

*The Eugene Barker History Center, Austin, Texas. A great collection of Texas history, newspaper microfilm, and helpful staff members. Research is a pleasure here.

*The late Ray A. Walter, *the* Limestone County historian. His knowledge of the people, and the history of the area set me back on the trail after many of my leads had grown cold. Much of the desired information on family roots; marriage records, probates, etc., were destroyed in two Limestone County courthouse fires in 1873. Fortunately, most land records were refiled to cure title, but the early personal records prior to 1873 will never be recovered. Ray Walter helped bridge the gap.

*The Waco-McLennan County Library has a magnificent collection of Texas and area history. Many hours of research here resulted in accumulation of valuable data, particularly court records. Thanks to Dan Haselett for his personal assistance.

*Thanks to the Texas Land Office at Austin, who provided the data, deeds and land history of the Austin colony and early Limestone County.

*Appreciation to my son, Gene, for his help with photos, editing and encouragement. Also my cousin, Lynda Lehmann French of Austin, who continued the Lehmann search while I branched off into other areas. My sister, Dorothy Lehmann Thomas, Muskogee; and Texas cousins; Billie Wallace Thomas, Dallas, and Alice Romberg, Dale, Texas, for their support.

*My newly discovered cousins: Joyce Angell, Cameron, Texas, who provided family photos of Louisa Lott, and the Aikman sons. Carroll Aikman, Meridian, Texas, whose knowledge of family history could have saved me lots of time had I found him sooner. He did confirm accuracy of my findings, and added new leads.

*Wallace descendants Effie Mae Bell, Killeen, Texas, who furnished information and photos of the W.W. Wallace family and Nell Wallace, Lorena, Texas, who did the same with the Robert Wallace family.

*The Oklahoma Historical Society and Archives. Their collection of history, manuscripts and documents is magnificent. Their staff is always eager to help.

*Pamela Puryear, my newly discovered Lott descendant cousin. What a jewel! Pam can leap over a locked gate and a five-wire, barb wire fence in a single bound. And she'll do it, too, in quest of family history. She needs only "a smidgeon," she says, in obtaining a doctorate in history from Texas A&M. She has studied and written Texas history, particularly about Austin's colony. Her ancestor grandfather, Robert A. Lott, built and operated the historic Austin House hotel at Washington-on-the-Brazos. He was a brother to my ancestor, John Lott, the hotel operator, and commissary of the Texas Revolution times.

Pamela still resides in her Youens ancestral home at Navasota, with her twenty-three kittens. The home, a beautiful two-story, was built in 1871 in the style of the Youens home at Dartford, Kent, England. It is listed with the Texas Historical Commission as a Texas Landmark.

Pamela discovered the Col. J.R. Cook grave and headstone in

1970. Cook's 1843 grave, in the old Farquahar Cemetery just outside old Washington, had been overgrown and hidden for decades by a dense growth of vinca major vines. The headstone has since been restored. You'll enjoy reading the J.R. Cook story, and several others enclosed herein, furnished by Pamela.

Lost Grave of Texas Hero Found By Pamela Puryear

At right: Pamela Puryear with rescued headstone of J.R. Cook

Pamela Ashworth Puryear (1943-2005) was a great-grand daughter of Robert A. Lott who operated a hotel at Washington-On-The-Brazos in the colonial and Republic era of early Texas. Obtaining a Masters Degree from Texas A&M College, she became an authority on the Victorian clothing of women in the period, and authored three books on history of the area, including "Sternwheelers and Sandbars," a history of travel and commerce on the Barazos River.

An original founder of the "Texas Rose Rustlers," she traveled the Austin Colony area seeking vintage roses the early settlers planted on homesteads and cemeteries. She would take cuttings from the roses and share with others and nurseries in propagating the roses. "Pam's Pink," and Climbing Pamela," varieties are named in her honor.

It was on a mission of rescuing vintage roses that Pamela discovered the long-forgotten grave of Col. James R. Cook in Farquhar Cemetery just north of Old Washington. Cook, a hero of battles at San Antonio de Bexar and at San Jacinto. Cook's grave was covered with underbrush and briar thickets that were practically impenetrable. Cook's headstone was cleaned, reset by stonemasons.

*And thanks to Catheryne McKeller, Hewitt, Texas, descended from Sarah Ann Lott and Hartwell Coleman Fountain, who furnished valuable Fountain family photos.

*Ora Posey Nielsen, of American Fork, Utah. What a blessing

to find her--a granddaughter of Bill Posey and Elizabeth Wallace! Just when all hope was gone of ever finding a descendant of Bill Posey my friend, Ray Walter came through again. He quizzed Posey descendants in Texas who furnished her name. This family history would not have been complete without material and photos furnished by Ora Posey Nielsen. Happily, it was a good exchange. I was able to supply her with the Wallace ancestry, of which she had no knowledge.

*The late Louise McIntyre, of White Oak, Texas, furnished much information on the Posey and Berryhill line in Alabama and Oklahoma. Such a gracious and beautiful lady! Her seven volumes of family history will hopefully go to the archives in Texas and Oklahoma for future generations to explore.

*And to Fred Olds; Western painter, sculptor, historian, illustrator, storyteller, and cherished longtime friend, my continued thanks for his help and encouragement.

CONTENTS

GONE TO TEXAS

Andrew Miller was born in North Carolina in 1785, the son of Henry Y. Miller, a Revolutionary War veteran, who had been born in Virginia and migrated to North Carolina before relocating to Tennessee. Andrew had relocated to Rapides Parish, Louisiana via Natchez and settled north of Alexandria on what was called "Island D," which was formed from two forks in the Red River. There he met and married Celia Neal, whose family had come to Rapides Parish from Georgia in 1810.

The Neal family was prominent in early Louisiana history. Celia's brother, Mitchell Neal had served in the Battle of New Orleans against the British in 1814 and was serving in the Louisiana house of representatives. Another brother, Thomas Neal was a Planter near Alexandria who spent a fortune in the Emancipation movement before the Civil War. Celia's sister, Coashti Neal-Dark, was a widow who ran a large plantation at Boyce, a few miles north of Alexandria.

Andrew Miller and Celia married in 1818 and soon had a daughter; Mary Cecelia was born to them in 1820. A son, Robert T. Miller followed in 1822. The Miller's continued their plantation operation on Island D, but Andrew's attention was being drawn to a new area. He had listened intently to Stephen F. Austin who told of his dreams of establishing a colony in the Spanish-owned land to the west called Texas.

Miller became enthused with the leadership of Austin and the projected opportunities in Texas. A colonist could receive a league of land (4,428 acres in Spanish measure), which was a generous allotment and incentive to relocate his growing family. Miller took the oath as an Austin colonist in 1822 and began making plans for relocation to Texas.

Texas had been vulnerable to Anglo settlement for years. Spanish government officials had tried unsuccessfully to establish Spanish-Mexican colonies in Texas to defend its north borders against intrusion by the Americans. Settlements had been established at Bexar (San Antonio), and as far north as Nacogdoches. None were successful. The proposal by Austin to settle Anglo families who would profess a loyalty oath to the Spanish government met with success and Austin was allowed to settle three hundred families in south-central Texas on the Brazos River.

Austin spent the summer of 1821 surveying the country in selecting a site for his colony. He went from Nacogdoches in the north to La Bahia, southeast of San Antonio, with a small party of Americans to pick his land. At Nacogdoches Austin noted there were only about three dozen Mexican inhabitants all told, with five houses and a church. He also noted some Anglo-American squatters, settlers who had moved across the Louisiana border and built cabins in the forest, on Spanish soil.

Stephen F. Austin

The small party traveled the Camino Real, or "Royal Road," which had been established by the Spanish in exploring the northern reaches of the country. The road was hardly more than a trail with the route being designated by hack marks on trees along the way. At an area where the Navasota River enters the Brazos, another route called the "Cushatta Trace" angled northeast toward Alexandria, Louisiana. Unsavory characters and pirates whose primary purpose was to move contraband goods in and out of the Spanish territory had hacked this route out. Both routes were extremely dangerous to travel, but a voyager was particularly vulnerable to attack by the thieves and cutthroats who lurked along the Cushatta Trace.

The most impressive region Austin found lay south of the Camino Real, between the Colorado and Brazos rivers. These rich river bottoms offered good rainfall, and it was accessible to the gulf where a cotton crop could be marketed and exported. Austin described the country as the best in the world with plenty of timber, fine water and rich bottomland. It was perfectly suited to the American plantation economy. The area lay outside the dangerous Indian country. It was inland from the foul-smelling and cannibalistic Karankawa Indians, and separated from the fierce Comanche tribes by a buffer of two somewhat-friendly Wichita tribes, the Wacos and Tawakonis.

It was over the Cushatta Trace that Andrew Miller rumbled in with two ox wagons of supplies and three Negro slaves. They had traveled with other settlers, including Miller's uncle, Andrew Ray, to afford protection against possible attack along the treacherous Cushatta Trace route.

The group set out through the wilderness driving their stock ahead of them, the traditional Kentucky rifle balanced in the crook of their arm to fend off attack by their own kind, or Indians that inhabited the area. Oxen pulled the wagons, straining as they went against the wooden bow that fitted over their necks. The land was rough. Every stream had to be forded. They would do well to make ten miles a day under the best of circumstances.

In the wagons were pens of chickens that would furnish eggs and meat when they were settled. Hogs and cattle were driven ahead that would comprise their brood stock. Horses and mules were also a part of the entourage. The wagon would carry other essentials; quilts, blankets, cast iron kettles and other house wares. Little, if any, furniture took up valuable cargo space in the wagons. Tables and benches would be constructed after arrival. The all-important double-bitted ax that was carried would be essential in setting up life on the new frontier.

With the ax, Miller would build the family's log cabin shelter and continue the tradition begun by his forefathers when they reached American shores. The ax would be used to fell the trees to build the structure, notching the ends in a dovetail for strength. The gaps between the stacked logs would be daubed with mud to keep out the winter chill. In summer the mud would be knocked out to allow a breeze to circulate air. But all cabins would eventually become what were called a "dog run" structure. It consisted of two separate cabin rooms on each end with a continuous roof connecting the two. The open corridor in

Typical Dog Trot House in Austin's Colony

between allowed for storage for harness, tools, saddles and other essentials needed at the homestead. Each cabin would have a chimney that would be constructed of mud-plastered rocks or sticks. The usual flooring was hard-packed soil. Later, logs would be leveled and laid down for the flooring. These cabins could be built with only an ax and a saw, and almost without the use of a single nail.

The ax would also be used to clear the woods, build the furniture and chop the wood for the fires that were a constant necessity. Food was cooked in the cast iron kettles and Dutch ovens. Clothing was washed in boiling water in cast-iron pots. A firewood pile around the cabin was essential, and must be maintained constantly. Once a fire was started it seldom was allowed to go out. The ax was also essential in building the split-rail stock pens to keep in the animals. Beef cattle could be allowed to roam. The land was good and the grass always green. There was little need for gathering hay except for the coldest winter months. The work animals, oxen and mules, were kept behind the split-rail enclosures or watched while they grazed.

The colonists had all taken the required oath of allegiance to the Roman Catholic Church and the Spanish government, which included the vow to take up arms in defense against "all kinds" of enemies; to be faithful to the King, and to observe the political institution of the Spanish monarchy. But Austin and the Spanish authorities had a clear understanding on two matters: one, that the American colonists would be substantial, law-abiding people; and

A typical farm scene in Austin's Colony in the 1820s

two, that the requirement of the Roman Catholic religion would not be enforced. Austin did keep up the requirements of character for his colony but not the religion.

Andrew Robinson became one of the first recorded settlers in Austin's colony, arriving in November 1821. Robinson and his son-in-law, Jack Hall, quickly built and began to operate a ferry just below a point south of where the Navasota River enters the Brazos River. Miller's league of land would be located adjoining the Robinson land, some four miles to the west, and located on Doe Run Creek, where the water was pure and plentiful. Andrew Miller crossed the Brazos River in January 1822, and took the oath required of Austin's colonists.

Austin had carefully chosen his colonists. He did not want frontiersmen or mountaineers. He did not want so-called "leatherstockings." The rules of his colony provided that "no frontiersman who has no other occupation than that of a hunter will be received--no drunkard, no gambler, no profane swearer, and no idler." These rules were enforced and he drove out of the settlement a number of families he deemed undesirable. On more than one occasion he ordered rules violators to be publicly whipped. Karankawa Indians who were caught pilfering supplies from the settlers were also whipped. The bewildered Indians were so taken aback at the method of punishment they did not return for a second helping of lashes at the stake.

Only a few of Austin's settlers were illiterate; most possessed some education. None were wealthy, but neither were they poor. Most brought some form of capital; seeds, equipment, stock or slaves. None of the colonists were large slave owners, but many owned some. Although slavery was not permitted under the Spanish or Mexican rule, the authorities agreed to accept their presence as "servants."

The first year of the colony, 1822-23, Austin was forced to stay in Mexico to defend his empresario commission before a succession of new, independent Mexican governments. The Mexicans had thrown over the Spanish government and it was necessary that Austin's contract be accepted by the new regime. After many trying circumstances and imprisonment by the Mexicans, Austin was finally granted permission to continue his colony. Other empresarios had been given land grants for a similar enterprise, but none were as successful as Austin's, and most were declared failures under the terms of agreement.

The economy of Austin's colony was mostly one of barter. Clothing made in Europe was traded for hogs. Horses were exchanged for corn, an ox for a sow, a feather bed for three cows with calves, a gun for a mare. These items were valued in dollars-and-cents, but money never changed hands. No one had any money. Taxes were paid in kind, at a rate of a cow and a calf for ten dollars.

The exports of the colony were cotton, beef, tallow, pork, lard, mules, etc. All these exports went to the United States, usually through New Orleans. The colony was so far from Mexico that little trading took place with their mother country. Slowly, an economy developed so that by 1832 a Mexican official listed Texas exports at $500,000. Cotton accounted for $353,000 of this--furs, hides and cattle the rest.

By 1824, Andrew Miller had developed his homestead on Doe Run Creek sufficiently to bring his family to the colony. Miller retained a close tie with his lands and family members in Louisiana, and made some trips back across the Cushatta Trace to retrieve supplies left behind. The trips were always made with other settlers, who could be assured of some degree of protection and safety in numbers as they traveled over the dangerous route. Arriving with Miller in 1824 was his spouse, Celia, and their children, Mary and Robert.

The colony continued to grow, and by 1825 counted 1,347 whites and 443 slaves living there. After Austin's first three hundred patents were used up, he applied for and was granted more. In ten years Austin located more than 1,500 American families. It was said that in a single decade, Austin's settlers had chopped more wood, cleared more land, broke more soil, raised more crops, had more children, and built more towns than the Spanish had in three hundred years.

The Andrew Miller family grew with the colony. In 1828, another son, Merideth Neal was born to the family, and another daughter, Lucretia, would be born in 1831. Like most settlers in the colony, the Miller's lost several babies in infancy. Disease was common in the early years, with pneumonia and fever claiming the most victims. It was said that after the first year a baby still had only a small chance for survival.

Arriving in Austin's colony in 1831, and settling on the Robinson survey was the family of John Lott. Lott, and his wife, Sarah Ann, brought with them a known son, John Lott, Jr., and two daughters; Sarah Ann, born in 1820, in Mississippi, and Louisa, born in 1828, near Tallahassee, Florida. The group also included five Negro slaves to help with the household, and to assist Lott with his anticipated business ventures in the new Texas home. Two of Lott's younger brothers, Dr. Arthur Lott and Robert A. Lott would join them later. Robert A. Lott arrived on Christmas day,

1836 and would build the Austin House Hotel that operated for many years at Washington-on-the-Brazos.

Their grandfather, John Lott I, of Celtic descent, had immigrated to America from Devonshire, England. He had first settled in North Carolina in 1745, but had drifted down to Georgia when it opened for settlement. He bought land in St. George's Parish and established a horse-breeding farm about twenty miles north of Savannah. He married a woman named Bethany, of half Cherokee blood, and was elected an assemblyman in the Georgia government. John Lott I, and Bethany had thirteen children, all named after Old Testament Biblical characters. John I, and the eldest son, John, Jr., both served in the Revolutionary War.

When central Georgia opened for settlement in the 1780s, some of the Lott families moved to Montgomery County. Further expansion of the westward movement saw many of them moving to Mississippi Territory where they settled in Marion County. Here John, Jr. settled and began a family. Among his children were John, born in 1790, Arthur in 1792 and Robert A., born in 1797. These three brothers located first in Florida, near Tallahassee, before moving on to Texas and a new home in the Austin colony.

Jack Hall had platted a new town to be located on the Robinson survey and began selling lots. He named the new town Washington-on-the-Brazos. John Lott bought two of the new town tracts and established a hotel, saloon and livery stable. Later he and Hall established a general merchandise store called Lott & Hall. The store quickly became the gathering point of the settlers in obtaining some necessities and gathering news.

The Anglo foothold in the Mexican province was gaining both economically and in population, but it was far from prosperous. Trouble was brewing in Mexico. Most Mexican government leaders distrusted the Americans. Many felt the immigrants had no real intentions of ever becoming loyal citizens of Mexico and their allegiance would always belong to the United States.

The Indian situation in Texas continued to be a frustration for the Mexicans. The single biggest reason for allowing Anglo immigration was to create a buffer between the colonists and the dreaded Comanches. Austin had wisely selected lands that placed the Wacos and Tawakonis between the colony settlement and the Comanches. The Comanches continued to harass the Mexican ranches near San Antonio and the Rio Grande however. The presence of the Austin Colony settlers to the east had proved to be no deterrent to Comanche depredations on the Mexicans. They were continually burned out, killed, or carried off by the raiding Comanche's.

A change in policy by the Mexican government toward the Anglo-Americans was blowing in the wind. It would soon reach hurricane proportions.

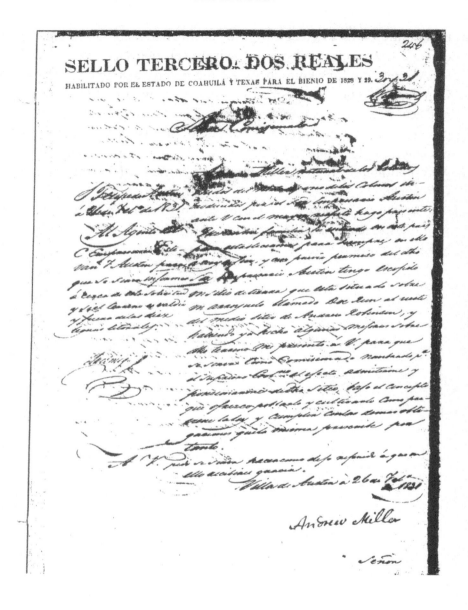

Mexican government land title grant to Andrew Miller For his League of Land as a member of Austin's Colony. The land located on Doe Run Creek was for 4,428 acres of Land and was issued February 26, 1831.

(Document on file at Texas Land Office, Austin, Texas.)

AUSTIN COLONISTS were granted a League and Labor of land as incentive to settle in early Texas. Andrew Miller arrived in Texas in 1824 receiving his League, 4,428 acres for stockraising. His application for the Labor of land, 177 acres for farming, was approved by the Washington County Board of Land Commissioners February 1, 1838, in Certificate No. 31, above. The land was located on Peach Creek in Brazos County, near present College Station, Texas. Miller was killed by Indians in March 1838, while inspecting the land after surveying. (Collection of Texas State Land Office).

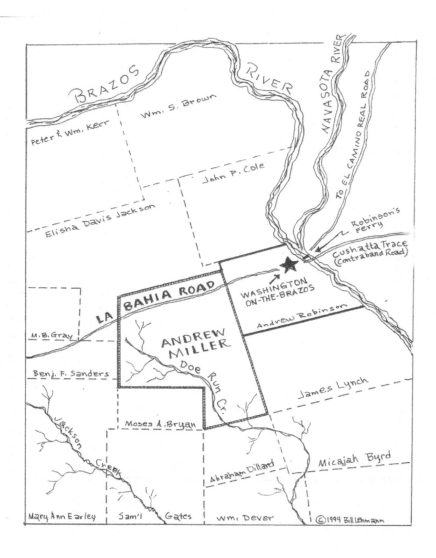

Map shows location of Andrew Miller's land near the capital of Austin's Colony at Washington-on-the-Brazos. John Lott's hotel, livery stable and commissary was the first sight that greeted visitors as they crossed the Brazos River into Washington.

BLOODSHED AT SAN ANTONIO

Trouble between the colonists and the Mexican government flared in late 1831. In this year, the state government at Coahuilla changed. The new governor reopened settlement under the old colonization law of 1825 to allow a number of latecomers to settle in southeast Texas, where they established a new town called Liberty. General Mier y Teran was outraged. Asserting military authority, he ordered a Captain Bradburn, who had built a fort at Anahuac, on Galveston Bay, to arrest the officials for issuing the new land titles. Bradburn, a particularly arrogant officer, exceeded his orders by marching troops into Liberty in May 1832, and officially abolished the community.

The action against Liberty caused a public complaint against the move and the contemptuous behavior of the Kentucky-born American, whom all the colonists despised. Bradburn answered by arresting several civilians, including William B. Travis. The prisoners were jailed in an old brick kiln. No charges were filed and Bradburn refused to turn them over to the civil authorities. The commandant at the Nacogdoches garrison, Col. de las Piedras heard of the troubles and arrived at Liberty with a handful of men. Realizing the situation was extremely volatile, and his forces were hopelessly outnumbered, Piedras agreed to negotiate. He promised to hear all grievances and have the prisoners turned to civil authorities. The action enraged Bradburn, who promptly resigned.

The action at Liberty prompted a skirmish between colonists under command of a John Austin, no relation to the empresario, and Mexican troops at Anahuac. A group of some 160 Anglos, unaware that a truce had been negotiated at Liberty, loaded three small cannon on a ship, and then sailed down the Brazos to attack Anahuac from Galveston Bay. However, a Mexican fort at Velasco blocked the armed schooner's passage downriver. The schooner stood off the fort, firing its cannon, while riflemen along its deck, sheltered by cotton bales, took devastating aim at the troops. In a short, but blazing firefight the colonists had blitzed the Mexican forces. Austin granted the troops the honors of war, and they marched off to Matamoros, across the border to Mexico. Then as Austin was readying his forces to attack Bradburn at Anahuac, word came that the crisis at Liberty had been averted, and Bradburn had resigned his commission and left the colony. Austin's army melted away and went back to their homes.

The skirmish would have caused instant retaliation under ordinary circumstances, but Mexico was having internal troubles of its own. A final crisis was delayed while the Mexican government went through a series of several upheavals. The showdown would be delayed for three more years. The skirmish was a signal that actual insurrection by the colonists was more than a possibility. It also showed that a strong wind of resistance to Mexican authority was blowing.

In April 1834, Mexican General Santa Anna took over the government. He dissolved the republican congress, dismissed all cabinet ministers and abolished all local legislatures and literally became King. Santa Anna despised the American colonists and suspected them of revolutionary intent. Austin had been summoned to Mexico City to discuss colony business. He met with Santa Anna, who insisted to Austin that 4,000 Mexican soldiers must be stationed in Texas for "the protection of the country." Austin argued that Texas was prepared to collect its taxes and guard its frontier without such government "assistance." Austin stood off the idea of additional Mexican troops while in the Mexican capital, and even secured Santa Anna's approval to admit more colonists.

Reasonably reassured, Austin wrote home stating that all was going well. He departed Mexico City and stopped over at the Coahuillan capital of Saltillo to conduct business with the Governor. He was suddenly arrested by presidential order and escorted back to Mexico City, where he was held incommunicado. The ruling would not allow him books, writing pens or paper, visits by friends, or even walks in the prison courtyard. He was kept in solitary confinement for several weeks.

Austin demanded a trial, but it was denied. News of his arrest caused great concern among the colonists in Texas. Two attorneys were able to raise money and petitions for Austin's release and they rode off into Mexico to present the papers. They succeeded only in having Austin released on bail on Christmas Day, 1834. The colonists were angered, but at Austin's insistence kept at their farming and stock raising. But things were changing.

Distressed by the deteriorating turn of events with the Mexican government, a call for a general convention at San Felipe de Austin to "discuss public safety" went out to the citizens. The message stated that the aim of the convention was to secure peace if it could be obtained on constitutional terms, and if not, to prepare for war. The convention also created a provisional government called the Consultation. The colonists were preparing for an inevitable break with the Mexicans. New towns in the expanding colony no longer carried Spanish names; they were now being called Columbia, Liberty and Washington.

Finally, on July 13, 1835, Stephen F. Austin was released after eighteen months of imprisonment. Santa Anna granted his boat passage to New Orleans, and Austin left Mexico with his trust in the Mexican government and Santa Anna completely destroyed. He was convinced now that Texas must separate from Mexico.

Arriving at New Orleans, Austin issued a call for help and urged Americans to bring arms and help in the impending struggle against the Mexicans. After issuing the call for help, Austin rode back across the Sabine to the Brazos. He reached San Felipe in September. He found matters far gone and a general feeling that war was imminent. A few days later, a courier rode hard all night bringing word that Mexican General Martin Perfecto de Cos was crossing the Rio Grande with a large army, bound for San Antonio. Austin now put out a call for Texans to stand to arms saying, "War is our only recourse. We must defend our rights, ourselves, and our country by force of arms."

Thus was created the very monster the Spanish and Mexicans had feared from the beginning. The colonists were preparing to revolt.

Austin assumed command of the colony forces as general. Couriers were sent out every dusty Texas trail, carrying the news and spreading alarm. Cos' troops arrived at San Antonio and immediately set about disarming the colonists. At Gonzales, the colonists had been issued a small, six-pounder cannon some years before to defend against the Indians. The Mexicans wanted it back and sent out a contingent of troops to bring it in. The colonists, hearing of the maneuver, buried the cannon and sent out runners calling for help.

On October 1, Captain Francisco Castenada arrived at Gonzales with fewer than 200 Mexican troops. He demanded the return of the cannon. The colonists, whose numbers had been bolstered by a steady stream of armed men coming into town, quickly dug up the cannon and mounted it on a wagon. They busily gathered up all kinds of scrap iron to be used as ammunition, put together a flag of white cloth and painted a picture of a cannon on the flag with the words: "COME AND TAKE IT."

On the morning of October 2, forces from both sides had been drawn up on the prairie. The colonists fired the Gonzales cannon without doing any damage. The Mexican captain asked for a parley, which was granted, but the two sides could reach no agreement. The colonist leader, John Moore, returned to his lines and ordered the Texans to open fire. A brief skirmish developed, but the Mexican forces immediately abandoned the field and marched off toward San Antonio. By now, word was out that there was shooting at Gonzales. There was no turning back now. The war had begun.

Stephen F. Austin arrived at Gonzales to assume command of the ragged Texan "army." Austin did not particularly want the job. He was no military man, and his health had been broken by the imprisonment in the Mexican jail. The group was headed for San Antonio. Some 300 colonists were goading for action, among them one Joseph Penn Lynch, who had joined the throng with his Kentucky long rifle.

Lynch had been drawn to Texas by other relatives who had

settled there. His uncle, James Lynch, had secured a league of land next to Andrew Miller, and called for young Lynch to seek his fortune in the new country. Joseph Penn Lynch was a dashing, young adventurer, born in Kentucky in 1810. He had arrived at Washington-on-the-Brazos in 1835, and quickly fit into the activities of the community, taking an active role in political affairs. He had come to Texas for excitement and he was about to get a full dose of it. Blood was about to spill on Texas soil.

The colonist "army" began moving slowly up the road to San Antonio. Leading the parade was the now-famous "Old Cannon Flag" of Texas. The Gonzales cannon, pulled by two yoke of longhorn steers, rumbled at the rear. But the famed cannon did not make it. Its wheels broke down and it was abandoned on the dusty, rough trail.

The Texans reached San Antonio and surrounded the little villa. The Mexicans, having faced the rifle fire of the colonists at Velasco had no desire to be a part of a repeat performance. They quietly stayed behind the walls. The Texans surrounded the town and were surprised at meeting no resistance. They began a waiting game with the Mexicans. They had nothing else to do. The crops were in, and they were content for a time. But the call for service had only been for two months, and half that time had already eroded away. Some grew restless and wanted to fight. Others quietly left and went back to their homes and families.

Austin was relieved of command at San Antonio and ordered to proceed to the United States where he was to appeal for aid from the Americans. He left on November 25. The troops held an election and the command was given to Edward Burleson, who carried the rank of colonel. On November 26, there was a sharp exchange between the forces. Cos' army was running out of hay for the animals. Some 50 foragers were dispatched to secure hay provisions, but the Texan forces killed all. The colonists were reluctant however, to continue an assault inside the city without artillery support. It was finally decided the forces would retire to their homes and give up the conquest at San Antonio. The baggage wagons had already been loaded, when a chance event would renew an interest to fight. A deserting Mexican officer was captured and brought before Burleson. During the course of interrogation in front of the Texan army, the deserter said Cos' army was disheartened, hungry and homesick. San Antonio could be easily seized, he told Burleson. Colonel Ben Milam, an old empresario agent issued a call for volunteers, and the Texans, who had been spoiling for a fight, quickly stepped forward. When Milam assembled his troops at an old mill just outside of town, he counted 301 volunteers. One of these was Joseph Penn Lynch, of Washington County, who was about to see his first action.

General Cos had divided his army into two divisions. One held the Alamo. The other was quartered to the west. Both divisions had artillery. The Texans had none. Milam's assault began at three in the morning, December 5. His men broke through the Mexican guards and into town. A bloody, house-to-house conflict now ensued and the Mexicans were being cleared by deadly firepower of the Texans. On the third day of the bitter fighting, Ben Milam was shot and killed. He was buried, with ceremony, in the courtyard of the house where he fell. Milam now became immortal, and the first of what would be a long line of Texas heroes.

The assault continued. Houses were reduced to rubble by the Mexican artillery. Few Texans were killed, but the toll of dead Mexicans continued to climb. Cos forces received reinforcements from the south, but his nerve was gone. He surrendered 1,105 officers and men, and his Alamo fortress on December 10, 1835. Burleson gave Cos the honors of war. He signed a covenant of surrender, and pledged not to ever fight the colonists again. He was allowed to march out of San Antonio and south across the Rio Grande into Mexico. Texas was now cleared of all Mexican soldiers.

Convinced the war was over at least until the following summer, the Texas residents in the army, including Joseph Penn Lynch drifted back to their farms and homes, but the Alamo had been occupied by the adventurous American backwoodsmen who had answered Austin's call for help with their long rifles, coonskin caps, deerskin clothes, and a will to fight.

WASHINGTON-ON-THE-BRAZOS

With the colonist revolt and military action against Mexico, Washington-on-the-Brazos suddenly found itself thrust into an important role in the colonial government. San Felipe de Austin had been the colonial center of government, perhaps because it was near Stephen F. Austin's home. There was no capitol building however because the Mexican government in far-away Saltillo controlled the colony. Knowing troubles with Mexico loomed on the horizon, the colonists hastily called a meeting to discuss future action. Thus was created the Colonial Consultation with delegates from all areas of Anglo-Texas, including Austin's colony.

Captain Jack Hall's town of Washington had shown some growth, and with the promise to build a meeting hall, the Consultation named Washington as the Anglo-Texan capital and moved into an unfinished building to discuss their future. A provisional government was created which consisted of a governor, lieutenant governor and a council. Henry Smith was elected governor. Stephen F. Austin, William H. Wharton and Branch D. Archer, the Consultation President, were appointed Commissioners to the United States.

The Consultation also appointed Sam Houston, late of Indian Territory and Tennessee, commander-in-chief of the army. Houston's "army" at San Antonio and Goliad consisted almost entirely of American volunteers. Only a handful of officers could legitimately call themselves Texans.

From the time of the earliest settlement the colonists had experienced trouble with the Indians. Most vulnerable were the horse herds of the settlers, which the Indians delighted in stealing. Families in the farthest reaches of the settlements were also targets of the Indians, and many were murdered in horrendous fashion. The depredations were of great concern and prompted the colonists to organize "ranging companies" to patrol settlement areas and to engage the Indians wherever they were found. The formation of these ranging companies was the birth of what would become the famed Texas Rangers to Texas history.

John Lott and his store at Washington-on-the-Brazos had been designated as a distribution point for the ranging companies to acquire shot, powder, horses and other supplies needed to quell Indian disturbances. Now that war with Mexico appeared imminent, the Consultation appointed Lott & Hall as a commissary and agent for the Texan army in addition to the appointment to supply the ranging companies.

Volunteers from the United States were streaming into Texas goading for action. Some answered Austin's call just for the adventure, but others were lured by the offer of free Texas land for their service. Most came overland to the Brazos River and the Robinson ferry. After crossing the Brazos on the ferry, the first sight that greeted the newcomers was the Lott & Hall establishment on the west side of the river. Several full companies of volunteers passed through Washington and were allowed to camp near the hotel when accommodations of the hotel were full up. Lott's hospitalities also included a saloon where the volunteers' thirst could be quenched with whiskey. Their horses were boarded at the livery stable and supplied with grain.

The tiny community of Washington was, like the rest of the Anglo settlements, very primitive. While Lott operated a hotel there, it offered no luxuries--just the bare necessities. The diary of William Fairfax Gray, a Virginia lawyer, told of his first encounter with Washington in a February 13, 1836 entry: "As we approached the Brazos, the road descended into a marsh of several miles extent, all subject to overflow. The trees showed marks of floods twenty to thirty feet high. The Navisot, or Navisota, as it is written on maps, lay on our right, and enters the Brazos opposite to the new town of Washington, which stands on the south bank. Arriving at the ferry we saw Capt. Sherman's company on the opposite bank, drawn up in order, and a crowd of citizens to receive them.

"We stopped at a house, called a tavern, kept by a man named

Lott, which was the only place in the city where we could get fodder for our horses. It was a frame house, consisting of only one room, about twenty by forty feet, with a large fireplace at each end, a shed at the back, in which the table was spread. It was a frame house, covered with clapboards, a wretchedly made establishment, and a blackguard, rowdy set lounging about.

"The host's wife and children, and about thirty lodgers, all slept in the same apartment, some in beds, some on cots, but the greater part on the floor. The supper consisted of fried pork and coarse corn bread and miserable coffee. Was introduced to Dr. Goodrich, a physician of the place and a member-elect of the new Convention. Found that Governor Smith was in San Felipe, and none of the government here. Resolved to go on directly to San Felipe. Dr. Goodrich gave me a letter of introduction to Dr. Stewart.

"Left Washington at 10 o'clock. Glad to get out of so disgusting a place. It is laid out in the woods; about a dozen wretched cabins or shanties constitute the city; not one decent house in it, and only one well defined street, which consists of an opening cut out of the woods, the stumps still standing. A rare place to hold a national convention in. They will have to leave it promptly to avoid starvation."

William Physick Zuber, a volunteer who passed through Washington on his way to join the Texan army described his visit in later years: "Arriving at the Brazos River, we noted only three good houses in the town of Washington-on-the-Brazos--all frame, and all in a row on the south side of Main street. John Lott's hotel was the first from the river. The second was a commercial house. The third was S.R. Roberts hotel. Beside these were only a few pole cabins. Our little company took quarters in the Lott Hotel, its proprietor being a commissary, whose duty was to feed and lodge volunteers enroute to the army."

Neither Gray nor Zuber were impressed with their entry into Texas. Their experiences after leaving Washington would be about the same wherever they went; the colony was only wilderness a few short years previously. There was some growth, but it was coming painstakingly slow.

The basic diet of the colonists was corn and pork in some form or other. One settler wrote: "we breakfast on hot corn bread and pork dressed in various ways. We dine at two on roast pork and corn bread, and at seven we sup on the same."

Wild game was plentiful in the colony, which included venison, buffalo, turkey, squirrel, rabbit and quail. Tea and coffee were the main beverages, but most coffee was made from roasted, or burned corn. Storekeepers did stock some whiskey, rum and brandy for those who were possessed of a little cash or something to barter.

The Consultation directed Lott to equip volunteers with needed supplies and direct them to San Antonio de Bexar. They promised Lott compensation for the services even though they had nothing more than faith that money could be raised for the impending action against Mexico.

A December 20, 1835, communication from Consultation delegate and fellow Washingtonian, Dr. B.B. Goodrich, to the legislative council told the body of the necessity to replenish the funds of Lott in supplying the volunteers. The letter stated it was impossible for Lott to procure provisions for the troops passing through Washington without some "immediate pecuniary assistance. Corn is scarce and high," the letter stated, "and cannot be purchased without cash. Such have been the heavy advances from his (Lott's) own purse to sustain the army on their march to San Antonio that his funds are exhausted, and nothing in the way of provisions can be purchased on the faith of the country," Goodrich's letter concluded.

Among volunteers passing through Washington was a company from Louisville, Kentucky whose captain, W.B.C. Wiggington, signed a voucher dated December 20, 1835, in the amount of $48.70 owed Lott for provisions. The company consisted of twenty-two men and four horses to the baggage wagon, said a note made by the captain on the voucher.

Following the victory of the colonists at San Antonio de Bexar, most drifted back to their homes to plan spring planting. They left the Alamo occupied mostly by the volunteers that had come in too late for action. The Consultation feared a retaliation following the defeat of the Mexicans. The appointment of Sam Houston as commander-in-chief added much faith and stability. Houston was now in Goliad plotting strategy for the feared Mexican invasion.

In a January 31, 1836, communication, the Consultation stated that the advisory committee was of the opinion that there was no further necessity in increasing the troops at Bexar (San Antonio). They sent an express rider with a message advising John Lott to direct all volunteers passing through Washington to proceed directly to Copano or Goliad, where the government supplies were stored. There they would receive orders for further movements from General Sam Houston.

Lott & Hall Store, Hotel, Tavern and Livery Stable

Brazos River

Drawing from Washington-On-The-Brazos State Park and Museum, Washington, Texas

OLD WASHINGTON AS IT WAS IN 1836

Independence Hall replica. This is where the declaration of independence and constitution for the Republic of Texas was framed in 1836.

WASHINGTON-ON THE-THE-BRAZOS STATE PARK AND MUSEUM

John Lott's Tavern was a popular place for citizens, especially during the constitutional convention being held across the street in Independence Hall. Here, re-enactor Donald Clark sits at the replica of Lott's Tavern. Clark was a great-great grandson of both John Lott and Andrew Miller. Austin colonists who resided at Washington-on-the-Brazos were part of early Texas history.

Donald Clark, re-enactor

THE FALL OF THE ALAMO

General Santa Anna was inconsolably enraged when Gen. Cos's troops returned to Mexico and told of their defeat at the hands of the colonists at Bexar. He had an army of more than 6,000 men in northern Mexico, above Saltillo. He rode into the city in mid-January, 1836, to organize the army for the advance into Texas to destroy the upstart American colonists once and for all. Santa Anna himself was going to lead the main force on a direct assault through San Antonio. He was not going to wait for an end to the winter rains. The defeat of Mexican forces at Bexar reflected on his honor and it must be restored.

Meanwhile, the Texans were planning an invasion of Mexico, despite their thin forces. Were it not for internal bickering among the leadership the plan might have gone forward with disastrous results. Houston had been appointed commander of the army, but he was not able to get some of the volunteers to follow his orders. The army of Texas was extremely small and was in total disarray. The colonial government was in even worse shape. Governor Smith was impeached on a vote of the Council but refused to vacate.

The Texans initially planned an invasion of Mexico at Matamoros while the Mexican army was in a state of retreat from the action at San Antonio de Bexar. Houston at first approved the plan, but decided against the bold action because of the thin forces of the Texans. Two adventurous captains: Johnson and Grant decided to proceed with invasion plans on their own. Most of the troops stayed with Sam Houston, but the upstart captains were successful in recruiting a hundred and fifty or so men to attempt the maneuver. Santa Anna was not asleep, however. He launched an offensive and had troops on the way to Texas the minute word reached him of the defeat of his forces at Bexar.

A small force of men went with Grant on a searching mission and met Mexican forces at Agua Dulce in late March 1836. All the Americans were killed. Grant himself suffered a horrible death when the Mexicans tied him to the tail and hind legs of a wild mustang horse they had captured. The horse, wild with fear, kicked Grant to death in trying to dislodge the foreign object that had been shackled to him. Johnson's forces reduced greatly when many went with Houston, encountered Mexican forces at Goliad. Most of the American forces were brutally killed. Johnson managed to escape.

The Alamo fortress was now under the command of Lt. Col. J.C. Neill, who complained to Houston that the facility had been stripped of its cannon, supplies and clothing for the aborted invasion of Matamoros. Neill also issued an urgent appeal for reinforcements. Houston dispatched Colonel James Bowie with a handful of men to march from Goliad to San Antonio on January 17. Houston trusted Bowie and wanted the veteran fighting man's assessment of the situation at the Alamo.

An army of some 500 men was now encamped near Goliad, and a few were garrisoned at the Alamo. Only about twenty five of these troops were actual Texans. The others had drifted in from all over the southern United States, passing through Washington-on-the-Brazos, and directed to San Antonio de Bexar by John Lott, the government agent. Some fifteen of the volunteers were citizens of the British Isles.

The Mexican general and president drove his troops forward from Saltillo at a feverish pace. They arrived at Laredo, on the Rio Grande, in mid-February, 1836. It was a remarkable pace, but a price was paid in a loss of hundreds of men and horses. More importantly, the winter rains had caused a quagmire on the trails forcing the abandonment of heavy artillery. The big guns followed, but far behind. When the Mexican troops pulled into sight of San Antonio, they had only two batteries of small six-pound cannons.

Santa Anna was somewhat surprised to find the Alamo defended. The population of Bexar, all Mexican, flocked to Santa Anna's side, giving him information about the North Americans holed up inside the Alamo. The force only contained a hundred and fifty men, he was told, and they were desperately short of gunpowder with which to fire the cannons that lined the walls. The citizens also told Santa Anna the Anglos had stripped the town of corn and driven thirty head of beef cattle behind the fortress walls. Santa Anna's cavalry wheeled into San Antonio on February 23, almost catching the Texans by surprise. They hadn't expected an arrival that soon, but had prepared a defense as best they could.

The Anglo-Texan government was still gripped in chaos, dissension and rivalry. The people of the colony were still mostly concerned with spring planting and private affairs. They had no idea the Mexicans were anywhere near with an army. The Alamo was now in a co-command of Bowie and Travis, and couriers were dispatched to appeal for reinforcements to help defend the fortress.

The couriers arrived in the Colorado-Brazos country shouting the alarm. Governor Smith tried to raise a force for the embattled Alamo, but the effort failed. He held title as governor, but actually held no power. Bowie had taken sick with pneumonia and directed his followers to obey the command of Travis.

Travis' command consisted of a conglomerate force of Americans, Scots, Englishmen, Texas-Mexicans and a few genuine Texans. They could have escaped the Alamo if they chose, but one hundred and fifty men stayed on to stubbornly fight an entire army, hopelessly awaiting reinforcements that never came. Travis had been trained at a military academy in South Carolina. He had been thrown out of school for inciting a student revolt, but had learned his military lessons well and had retained them in his memory.

Travis had come into Texas as a lawyer in the early Austin colony era. He made entries daily in a diary he kept religiously. The diary he kept during the siege of the Alamo would delight historians and give valuable insight into the events that took place before and during the battle. Travis did considerable traveling around colonial Texas attending to legal affairs. One entry in his diary of August 30, 1833 noted that he had visited a client at Washington-On-The Brazos, stating "I left San Felipe in company with G. Huff on Huff's mule. Dined with Edwards. Huff paid. Staid (sic) all night at Andr. Miller's."

Bowie was raised into wealth in Louisiana in the early 1800's.

He was schooled, but sought adventure and found it. He was equally at home in the highest society to the lowest of cutthroats and was held in high esteem by both. He ran slaves with the pirate Jean Lafitte, explored Texas, and fought Indians. He had killed several men, including Lafitte's own son who had betrayed him.

He had his brother, Rezin, forge a huge knife he had designed, which he carried in his belt. The knife, which quickly caught on with the frontiersmen, was named "The Bowie Knife." It became a part of the standard frontier armament and was even manufactured in England for a time.

The Alamo Complex in 1836

After a bloody feud in Louisiana in which he and his huge knife continued the legacy, Bowie drifted into Texas. He quickly entered Spanish society and married the beautiful daughter of the Vice-Governor of Texas, Ursula Veramendi. He became owner of several leagues of land and became quite wealthy. In a great cholera epidemic that struck San Antonio in 1833, Bowie lost his wife, an infant son and a daughter to the disease. He had had no contact with the Texas colonists before this time but had known Sam Houston before. With his ties to Mexico gone, Bowie fell into the Texas Revolution through Houston. It was Houston who dispatched Bowie to the Alamo because of his great respect and trust.

David Crockett was already a living legend of the Frontier times as he entered Texas and became absorbed in the impending fight at the Alamo. He also was a frontiersman, born in the state of Franklin before it became Tennessee. Crockett's father had fought against the British. Crockett was never a farmer or businessman. He was always a hunter and trapper. He did enter politics in Tennessee at one time and served a term in Congress. But he came into opposition with Andrew Jackson, President of the United States. Crockett opposed the forced removal of the "civilized" Indian tribes, which infuriated Jackson. Since the President controlled patronage, he easily had Crockett defeated at the polls. Crockett made a short concession speech to his constituents in which he told them they could all go to Hell. He then headed south to Texas.

Crockett and four volunteers passed through Washington-on-the-Brazos January 24, 1836, spending the night at Lott's hotel, getting supplies and instructions. Before departing, Crockett signed a voucher certifying "John Lott furnished myself and four other volunteers on our way to the army with accommodations for ourselves and horses. The government will pay him $7.50," the document concluded. Crockett and his friends left Washington January 25, 1836, and were behind the walls of the Alamo when the Mexican troops wheeled into position.

Santa Anna's troops had been kept busy hurling fussilade-after-fussilade at the walls of the Alamo. The Texans had been under ten days of siege. Couriers came and went from the Alamo. James B. Bonham, courier and honorary

General Santa Anna

colonel had made several dangerous trips to the outside seeking help for the beleaguered Texans. He begged Fannin at Goliad to move his troops west. No help came and none was promised. Thirty-two Texans gathered at Gonzales and rode to the Alamo, where they had to fight their way inside to join the other forces. Bonham kept up his forays and appeals to the bitter end. Even when he was on the outside for the last time, knowing the end was near for the men at the Alamo, Bonham turned his horse back west and rode to his impending death.

The Texans were unable to mount an effective cannon counter battery because of the lack of gunpowder. Their nighttime raids behind enemy lines had some effect, but they would not result in any devastating damage. The rifle fire had been effective but again would only make a small dent in the thousands of Mexican troops surrounding the defiant Texans.

Santa Anna was growing impatient. He knew The Anglos were meeting again on the Brazos. He also knew that no resistance could challenge his army after he put down the defense at the Alamo. He had been able to work his artillery into a closer position and had knocked a breach in the east wall of the fortress. Finally, on March 5 Santa Anna called for an all-out assault on the Alamo.

Five battalions of some 4,000 men assembled in the chilly pre-dawn hours of March 6 to begin the ordered assault. Santa Anna had run up a blood-red flag on the highest flag pole telling the Texans they would be given no quarter. The Mexican army, marching in regiments with bayonets flashing, approached the fortress. The Tennesseeans; the Kentuckians; and the other frontiersmen-marksmen seldom missed. Their long rifles were effective at long ranges. The rifle fire from behind the Alamo began taking down the Mexicans column by column. It was an American tradition to shoot at the braid of the officers, and they began falling out, dead and wounded. The first assault by the Mexican troops never reached the walls.

The Mexicans kept coming. Finally, some columns reached the walls, and ladders went up. They quickly came down as the deadly rifle fire took its toll on the troops. But still they came. Ladders again went up against the walls, and this time they stayed. The Mexican soldiers went into the foray in hand-to-hand combat. One by one the defenders fell, ringed by the many Mexican soldiers who fell around them. Sheer numbers finally overpowered the defenders.

At nine o'clock, March 6, 1836, five hours after it began, the assault on the Alamo was over, and it had fallen. All the Texans had been killed, their bodies mutilated, and later burned on huge brush fires built on the orders of Santa Anna.

The Mexicans paid a heavy price in achieving the victory. Of the eight hundred men engaged in the first assault, six hundred and seventy had been killed. The other battalions had lost an estimated twenty five percent of its force. In all, there were nearly 1,600 Mexican dead. When Santa Anna was again able to march he left behind some five hundred wounded. Alcalde Francisco Ruiz of San Antonio was placed in charge of burning the Texan bodies. His official count was exactly one hundred eighty two. The charred remains of the Alamo dead were dumped into a common grave. Its location was not recorded and has never been found.

A Negro slave, Mrs. Dickenson, and several Mexican women and children were the only survivors of those behind the Alamo walls. They were expressly saved on direct orders of Santa Anna. They were released and made their way east and into the lines of the Anglo-Texans, where Santa Anna hoped their tale of the Alamo massacre would spread fear throughout Texas. Their story would not be told to colonist-Texans however, for they had declared Independence on March 2, 1836, and were ready to fight and die for their new Republic.

The colonist convention was held at the newly designated capital at Washington-on-the-Brazos beginning March 1, 1836. Sam Houston had attended as a delegate from Refugio. He was instrumental in keeping the convention on the course of its business. Now that the delegates had declared independence from Mexico, the next step was to draw up a constitution. The Texas

Constitution was hastily drawn up, and was a composite of the constitutions of both the Union and several of the Southern states. The Convention of fifty-nine delegates adopted the document on March 16. Sam Houston had been appointed again as Commander In Chief of the army. This time the commission spelled out complete power to command all forces and men in Texas, regular or volunteer.

Sam Houston had come into Texas December 10, 1832, from the Indian Territory where he had lived since 1829. He first dabbled in real estate then got caught up in the events of the Texans. Houston had been a U.S. Congressman and Governor of Tennessee, and was quickly sought out for his leadership and wisdom in political affairs.

He was born in Virginia March 2, 1793, the son of a plantation and slave owner. His father died when Sam was a young boy. He was rebellious in his youth and had a disdain for education. Houston was serving an apprenticeship in a dry goods store when he decided to run away from home. He was gone several weeks before his brothers found him living with a band of Cherokee Indians. He remained with the band for three years. The experience would cause him to champion the cause of the Indian in his later political roles.

The Hiwassee band of Cherokees, numbering about three hundred, were led by Chief Ooleteka--called John Jolly by the whites. Young Sam was adopted by the chief and given the name Kalanu, or "The Raven," a name that would follow with him throughout his life. In 1820 Ooletka became Principal Chief of the entire Cherokee Nation.

Leaving the Cherokees, Houston was drawn into the Creek War, serving with Andrew Jackson. The alliance would form a lasting friendship and trust. In a fight with the Creeks at Tohopeka, Houston would receive two wounds from rifle balls to his right shoulder. The wounds would leave disfiguring scars and troubling pain the rest of his life. Jackson became governor of Tennessee, took an interest in Houston and began guiding his career. In the autumn of 1817 Jackson asked Houston to talk to his friends, the Cherokees, and persuade them to move to the newly designated lands of Indian Territory.

Jackson then guided Houston into law, and he began studies with Judge Trimble at Nashville in 1818. After a few months of intensive study, Houston was admitted to the bar and began practicing law. Jackson next guided his protégé into politics and Houston was elected to Congress in 1823. His popularity and leadership increased under Jackson's tutelage, and Houston was elected Governor of Tennessee in 1827.

Houston's career soared. Many believed his destiny would someday take him to the White House as president under Jackson's guidance, who was himself now president. Then a strange turn of events would spell disaster to his career. Houston fell in love with Eliza Allen, many years his junior, and the couple was married January 22, 1829. After only three months and one day of marriage Eliza left him. Some said the age difference was too much. Others said she was repulsed by Houston's disfiguring shoulder scars suffered in the Indian wars. The real reason was never revealed, but it was devastating to Houston's promising career. He resigned as governor on April 16, 1829, and left Tennessee to join his Cherokee friends in the Indian Territory.

Houston arrived by steamboat at Fort Gibson, which had been established April 22, 1824, to protect the Indian tribes from one another. It became the western terminus for the removal route of the Indians that was known as the "Trail of Tears," due to the many deaths and suffering by the Indians as they traveled the route to their new home. The fort was located on the forks of three major rivers in the Territory; the Verdigris, Neosho and the Arkansas.

On September 21, 1829, Houston became a citizen of the Cherokee Nation, and opened a trading post near the Fort Gibson garrison, which he called "Wigwam Neosho." Chief Jolly, representing the Cherokee Nation, soon appointed him Ambassador to the United States. He went to Washington January 12, 1830, to visit his old friend, President Andrew Jackson, and became a regular visitor there. Jackson always welcomed him, but he never got used to Houston's eccentric style of dress: Buckskin leggings, moccasins, brilliant Indian hunting shirt and distinctive Cherokee turban.

Houston married again in the summer of 1830, this time to Tiana Rogers Gentry, also called Diana and Talahina. She was the daughter of John Rogers, a Scottish trader. Her mother was one-eighth Cherokee, making Tiana one-sixteenth Cherokee blood. Her uncle, Ooletka, was chief. Houston had met the family during his early stay with the Hiwassee band. Tiana was the widow of a white blacksmith named David Gentry. She was a striking woman, intelligent and educated. She had been privately tutored at home and had attended formal schools in Tennessee. She had property, livestock and slaves. Houston and Tiana would remain together for the remainder of his time in the Cherokee Nation.

During his years among the Cherokees, Houston would meet many explorers who came to Fort Gibson before embarking on their exploration of the lands that lay to the west. The fort was the farthest outpost west of the Mississippi River at the time, and little was known about the country or the people west of the fort. One of Houston's acquaintances was Jesse Chisholm, who was a regular visitor. Chisholm was part Cherokee, and was held in high esteem by both the Indian and the whites. He regularly traversed the western areas of the Indian Territory, and traded with the so-called "wild tribes" west of the fort.

Houston had traveled to Washington many times to visit with his friend Andrew Jackson. In Washington he was kept abreast of the developments in Texas between the Mexicans and the Texans. President Jackson had a keen interest in the affairs, perhaps feeling that Texas would eventually win freedom from Mexico and become a state. Houston, perhaps at the urging of Jackson, decided to leave the Cherokees and head for Texas. He was issued passport August 6, 1832.

Before leaving Wigwam Neosho for Texas, Houston noticed a visitor coming into the fort, having just arrived by steamboat. The commandant at Fort Gibson, Col. Matthew Arbuckle had invited the noted author, Washington Irving to accompany a group on an exploratory mission in the western Indian Territory. Houston met Irving and took a ride with him and Col. Arbuckle to Chouteau's trading post, some thirty miles north of the fort.

Irving had sought permission to make the trip, where the exploration party hoped to come in contact with the plains tribes, particularly the Comanches, in establishing peace between the tribes and the settlers moving west--Indian and white. Irving would pen his famous "Tour Of The Prairies," and the adventures of the group. They saw only a small hunting party of Osages on their six-week journey. They never made contact with the Comanches, but were probably watched on the entire route by the eyes of those whom they sought.

Houston left Wigwam Neosho and Fort Gibson in mid-November, 1832, heading down the Texas Road to Fort Towson, on the Red River. After stopping at the fort for several days, he finally crossed the Red River and into Texas on December 10, 1832. He entered Texas at Jonesborough, and then made his way to Nacogdoches and San Felipe, where he would become a famous part of Texas history.

The events at the Alamo spurred the men of the colonies into action. They no longer doubted the possibility of war. It was here, and it was now. They only knew the Mexicans had surrounded the Alamo, but they knew it was time for action.

Joseph Penn Lynch, of Washington-on-the-Brazos had served the colonial army from July 9 to August 31, 1835, as a member of Captain Philip Coe's Company of Rangers. He was officially cited for his participation in the storming and capture of Bexar, from December 5 to 10, 1835, during his term of enlistment from October 1 to December 22, 1835.

Lynch answered the call to arms again and enlisted for service at Washington-on-the-Brazos March 1, 1836, one day before the Declaration of Independence was announced by the delegates to the convention. Lynch was given the rank of Captain and recruited a company of volunteers in Washington municipality in March 1836. The company went under the command of Lieutenant Colonel Somervell, commander of the First Regiment, Texas Volunteers.

With the convention still in session at Washington, Houston hurried to Gonzales, which was still the marshaling point for the decimated Texan army. He arrived on March 11, and there he found a total of 374 men, with no food, and some without arms and ammunition. The men had assembled without leadership, to help Travis at the Alamo. The best of these was a force of 50 Kentucky rifles Sidney Sherman had brought at his own expense from the United States. Houston organized this group into a regiment with Edward Burleson as colonel and Sherman as lieutenant colonel. At best, the future of Texas looked extremely bleak.

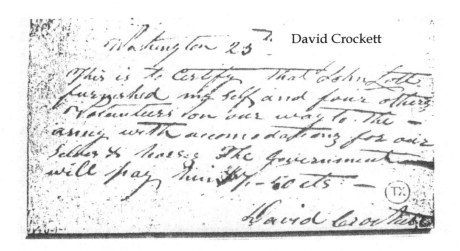

David Crockett

David Crockett's voucher issued to John Lott January 25, 1836. The fabled Crockett would die at the Alamo in March.

Texas State Library and Archives collection, Austin

David Crockett and four Tennessee volunteers passed through John Lott's commissary on their way to the Alamo at San Antonio. His voucher to the Republic of Texas verified payment of $7.50 for services rendered the party. All would die in the battle of the Alamo. Crockett, David Bowie and the others became legendary heroes in Texas history.

BATTLE FOR INDEPENDENCE

Gonzales was in a state of fear. On March 11 a Mexican had come into town and announced that the Alamo had fallen. Houston had just arrived, and hearing the report, sent three of his scouts, "Deaf" Smith, Henry Karnes and R.E. Handy, riding west for news. The scouts found Mrs. Dickenson and the bedraggled female survivors of the Alamo struggling down the road and brought them into town. Houston and the townspeople heard the tragic news of the horrible deaths of the gallant men. Also listening were the 20 widows and 100 children of the Gonzales men who had been slain after fighting their way into the Alamo to help in its defense.

The women also told Houston that Mexican General Sesma was close behind and his troops were advancing to destroy the Anglos. Houston knew his regiment was small, completely untrained and undisciplined. He chose to begin a retreat until reinforcements could be added and training could be provided. Geographically, the area was barren, but Houston also wished to pull the Mexicans into Anglo-Texas, where its numerous rivers and trees would provide a better defensive posture.

Houston penned a message to Fannin at Goliad with instructions to blow up the fortress, retreat, and meet him with his needed 500 troops. Houston then set fire to Gonzales and marched his hungry, bedraggled soldiers northeast. He reached Burnam's Crossing on the Colorado River on March 17. By now his army had grown to over 600 men. He halted nine days and taught his troops to drill. On March 28, he marched further north and reached San Felipe, the former colonial capital on the Brazos River. He camped for ten days at Groce's Plantation where the troops were given additional training. By now, the call to arms had produced an army of 1,400 men. The old colonists were now citizens of the brand-new Republic of Texas and responded by furnishing supplies and other goods to the troops. Among those was Andrew Miller, who furnished beef from his herd stock.

Meanwhile, Colonel Fannin at Goliad sent one third of his

forces to Refugio, a nearby town, to assist the evacuation of the Anglo settlers whom he had advised to flee. This force was gobbled up quickly by the advancing Mexican troops and slaughtered. Some escaped to the woods, but the Mexicans took Refugio and headed for Goliad. Fannin awaited reports from the command at Refugio, and finally word arrived that the force had been defeated. Fannin then decided to move his remaining troops to Guadalupe Victoria, but by now the Mexicans were in contact. He then decided to abandon the fortress at La Bahia and take his chances in the open country. His army, covered by a ground fog, moved out of the fortress on March 19.

The sun soon blazed away the fog shroud and left the troops fully exposed and vulnerable to the Mexican guns. Fannin's transport animals had been burdened by heavy guns and were weak. Some of the officers wanted to try and make it to a nearby creek, where a defense could be more easily arranged. The Mexicans began firing their guns at the retreating troops before they had time to reach shelter. They were in the open and away from water. They fought a creditable battle until the sun went down, but Fannin was unnerved by the sounds of his wounded troops crying for water. At daylight the Mexican guns began spraying the Texans with grapeshot inflicting more casualties. Fannin knew the situation was hopeless, so he raised the white flag of surrender believing he and his troops would be afforded the honors of war, and exiled to the United States.

If Fannin had known that Santa Anna would offer no quarter and would not extend the honors of war to his troops, it is doubtful he would have surrendered. But the Mexican general was determined to rid Texas of all Anglos, and he gave orders to slaughter all the troops. 390 Americans were executed, including Fannin. 27 had managed to escape, some being helped by a Mexican colonel named Guerrier, a professional soldier who believed Fannin's men should have been accorded war honors and allowed to leave. Santa Anna's action at the Alamo and at Goliad made martyrs of the slain Texans. The incensed Houston kept drilling his recruits awaiting his opportunity to meet the Mexican general on the battlefield.

At the end of March 1836, Santa Anna was supremely confident that the Texan army had been broken and his mission now was merely to search and destroy. His combined five divisions now swept toward the Sabine River intent on destroying everything in its path. Their orders were to burn every town, plantation, farm and dwelling. The presence of the Anglo in Texas was to be erased forever.

A great evacuation of the Austin's colonists began when word reached the villages that the Mexicans were advancing, killing and destroying everything in sight. The seat of government now moved from Washington--The-Brazos to Harrisburg on Buffalo Bayou, near Galveston Bay. Most of the population of Anglo-Texas, horrified and frightened at the tales of Mexican atrocities, was deserting the countryside ahead of the advancing troops. Most able-bodied Texas men, including many boys were joining Houston's army.

Andrew Miller sent Celia, the children, and several of their slaves east toward Louisiana and a safe haven with relatives. The little town of Washington was mostly deserted but John Lott was still directing incoming volunteers to Houston's forces. Andrew Miller stayed at his homestead determined not to leave until he had to.

The rainy season had hit Texas. The rivers were overflowing their banks, and all trails were seemingly bottomless mud pits. Soon the ferries were jammed with the fleeing settlers, who were leaving with all the valuables they were able to load. Wagons broke down, and possessions began to litter the muddy roadways as the frantic settlers struggled toward the east. The smoke of the Mexican destruction was rising behind them, as farm after farm was set ablaze.

The families of the Mexican officers and men were allowed to follow their troops. They remained at the rear, but were permitted to plunder and gather the spoils of war. A courier message from a

Mexican general named Gaona told Santa Anna that his brigade found dwellings of the settlers so well supplied that neither the officers or the soldiers had any more space to carry furniture and effects and were being forced to abandon the newly-acquired treasures.

Sam Houston kept up his retreat, passing the town of San Felipe on the Brazos River. He left behind a small force at the crossing, ordering them to hold it as long as possible. With the bulk of his army, Houston crossed the Brazos and headed on south. Santa Anna, getting wind of the direction of Houston's retreating army, turned his troops south in pursuit, thus sparing many of the farms that lay to the north and east of San Felipe. He seized the ferry at Fort Bend, and getting word that the government was now located at Harrisburg, turned his troops east to capture the town. The president of the new Republic, David Burnet, just barely got away before the invading troops arrived. They burned Harrisburg to the ground. The army then turned to the town of New Washington, on the bay, and then swung back northwest to the San Jacinto River.

Hundreds of volunteers had tired of Houston's retreating tactics and had left to go back and help their families in evacuation. With the Mexican army closing in, Houston was running out of time and space. He had trained his army to a perfect pitch. They were tired and angry, and wanted to fight. Houston had retreated from the Brazos to Harrisburg, left his sick and disabled in the ruins, and then sprung his troops into position between the San Jacinto and Buffalo Bayou. He was now ready to fight.

On April 20 Santa Anna found Houston's ragged forces. A light skirmish ensued, but Santa Anna did not attempt to drive the battle home. He awaited reinforcements. Santa Anna's brother-in-law, and the loser of the December battle at San Antonio, General Cos, arrived with 400 men to join Santa Anna's force of 800. The Mexican forces now outnumbered Houston's, who had arrived with only 918. Santa Anna grew contemptuous of Houston and felt no need to begin the battle. He camped about three quarters of a mile from Houston's position and built a fortification of saddlebags and brush.

In the skirmish before the main battle, a horse ridden by a young lieutenant, James R. Cook, became frightened by the sound of cannon, bolted and ran, unfortunately, for the Mexican lines. Cook had purchased the green-broke horse for the sum of $25.00 only a few weeks before. He bought the animal from John Lott, his future father-in-law, and the commissary at Washington-on-the-Brazos. The frightened horse dashed toward the Mexican lines, jumped the piles of breastwork-brush, and planted himself and the young lieutenant right in the middle of the Mexican enemy.

Cook, seeing no way to escape a terrible fate, dug his spurs into the animal's flanks and ordered the horse to "charge." The Mexicans were as startled as Cook and his horse at the surprise visit, but fired a few departing volleys at the horse and rider as they bolted over the brush barricades and dashed back toward the Texan lines. The Mexicans could hardly have missed such an easy and close target, but the fear of hitting one of their own caused them to check up their aim, it was reported by Cook's commanding officer, Capt. Henry Karnes.

Houston held a war conference with his commanders at noon on April 21. He had planned an attack on the morning of the 22nd, but every company of his command voted to fight immediately. The Mexican army was taking a siesta in the shelter of the trees. Santa Anna had also retired to his tent, perhaps thinking about the battle he thought would be fought the next day, but more intent on the amorous adventure that lay ahead with one of the women he had brought along from Mexico.

Deaf Smith and some handpicked trusted men had been sent to destroy Vince's Bridge across the Brazos a few miles away. It cut off the Mexican retreat, but it also trapped the Texans if they should lose. They could now only conquer Santa Anna's army or die.

Houston organized his troops for a three o'clock attack. They were positioned and given the command to move forward. The tired, dirty, hungry and angry Texans leveled their long rifles and advanced across the swampy plain. Catching Santa Anna's troops by complete surprise, the Texans began killing the Mexicans while shouting "Remember The Alamo! Remember Goliad! Remember The Alamo!"

Houston was at the head, leading the great charge against the still-drowsy Mexican forces. The Texans swarmed the barricades, their rifles cracking, Mexicans falling dead and wounded upon the trampled ground. The Mexicans, caught by total surprise, could not reload, could not

Gen. Sam Houston

form a defense and could not wield the bayonet. Houston's great horse, Saracen, was shot from under him. He quickly grabbed a new mount from an aide and continued leading the battle.

The battle lasted only a few minutes. The mopping up action took longer. The enemy troops were in a rout and fleeing for their lives. Retreating in a panic, hundreds of the soldiers found their path blocked by a deep ravine or a bayou. Some fled to the open prairie, but were quickly chopped down by the Texans. Houston's second horse was shot from under him, and this time the general caught a rifle ball in the ankle. The rout continued, but in the confusion of the battle Santa Anna, and his brother-in-law, Cos, had escaped capture.

That evening, Houston sat under a large, spreading live oak tree hearing reports. His boot was full of blood from the ankle wound. The Texans had counted 630 dead enemy troops scattered around the field of battle. About the same number had surrendered, some 200 of them wounded. They sat on the ground still dazed by the horror and swiftness of the battle. Amazingly, the Texans lost only two killed in action. Seven more would die later from the ranks of the 30 that had been wounded.

On April 22, the day after the battle, the Texans brought in Santa Anna, the Mexican general and president, who having disguised himself as a lowly unranked soldier, was trying to sneak behind the Texans lines and escape back to Mexico. The patrols also rounded up his brother-in-law, General Cos.

Houston's ankle wound required treatment. He was in agony and must sail to New Orleans to have the wound attended. Before leaving, he had Santa Anna write orders to the officers in his command to retire the troops to San Antonio, pending a total cessation of war and the negotiation of peace with the new Republic of Texas.

Houston then turned his high-ranking prisoner over to President David Burnet and left Texas for medical attention. On May 14, 1836 at Velasco, Santa Anna signed a public treaty with the Republic of Texas. He agreed to end all hostilities between the two nations at once. The Mexican army in Texas would withdraw below the Rio Grande, and all Texas prisoners still held would be released.

Invoice from Lott & Hall to Republic Of Texas for supplies
and services rendered volunteers during the Texian Revolution against Mexico. David Crockett & Co. is 13th on list.
Charge for J.R. Cook's horse is 18th on list.
(From the Texas State Archives Collection, Austin).

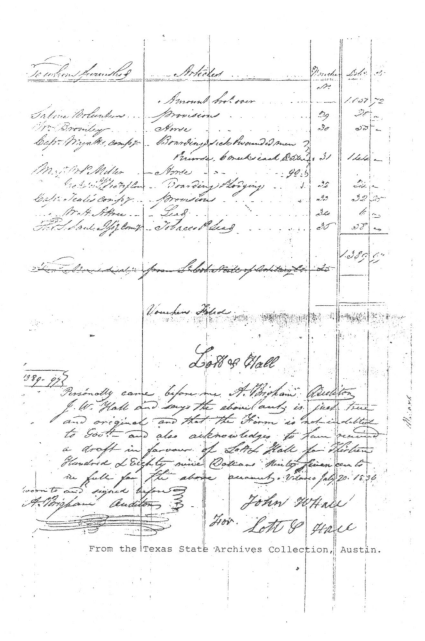

From the Texas State Archives Collection, Austin.

A NEW LIFE IN THE NEW REPUBLIC OF TEXAS

Hardly had the sun set over San Jacinto before the Texas farmers in Houston's army began to drift away, back to their farms and families. They were not soldiers but had agreed to fight only for the current emergency. They had crops to tend. They had rebuilding to do from the destruction inflicted on the property by the Mexican soldiers.

Within a few weeks, virtually every soldier had departed for home and family. Among them was Captain Joseph Penn Lynch. His first order of business was to find Mary Miller, the daughter of Andrew and Celia, and ask her to be his bride.

The Mexican invasion and chase of Houston's army through the Austin colony had caused initial panic and pandemonium. But the people themselves quickly reestablished a sense of order. The vast majority of the citizens fleeing ahead of the Mexican troops immediately turned around and went back to their farms even before it was certain the Mexicans had been defeated.

Celia Miller, her children and the slaves returned to find Andrew Miller already getting everything back in order. The Mexican army had turned south in their pursuit of Houston, and the homesteads around Washington-on-the-Brazos had generally been spared. Some damage had occurred in the area, but it was by Texan looters on there way east and out of reach of the Mexican army. Miller's homestead on Doe Run Creek had not been touched. The family was now back, and life could begin anew.

Joseph Penn Lynch, after discovering the Miller family, and Mary, were safe, returned to his military company to finish out the remainder of his three-month enlistment term. He was honorably discharged May 30, 1836. He hastened home to Washington where he and Mary Miller were married. He was soon elected as an Alcalde for the county of Washington, and began thinking about the future. He was to be allotted substantial acreage to compensate his service to the colony and Republic during the time of emergency.

The government of Texas had no money during the revolutionary period. Now that it had won independence Texas was even in debt on money borrowed. There never was money to compensate its army. With independence, Texas was issuing a general call for settlers, hoping to eventually be admitted as a state in the Union. The rewards to its former servicemen and enticement to new settlers was land--of which it had plenty.

Texas noted with sadness and respects the death of Stephen F. Austin at the plantation of his sister at Peach Point, near San Felipe on December 27, 1836. Many said the time spent in the Mexican prisons, and the subsequent Revolution had taken its toll on his health. But there was hardly time to mourn the death of the former empresario, for there was a building economic crisis. Cotton was selling for a mere 15 cents per pound. Flour was $6.00 per barrel; corn 50 cents a bushel and pork 6 cents per pound. Whiskey, if you had the money to buy it, was 36 cents per gallon.

An illustration of a return to normal times was an advertisement in the newspaper placed by a P.R. Splane, dated October 17, 1836, challenging any and all lovers of the sport of turf to a horse race. Splane's advertisement said: "I will run against any horse, mare or gelding that can be produced at my place, known as the Gin Place, six hundred yards or one mile, agreeable to the rules of racing, for any named sum of ten thousand dollars or under."

There was a greater desire on the part of the discharged volunteers who possessed considerably less than $10,000, and had only a slow horse, to have their land located and surveyed. The original empresario allotments had all been assigned, and new lands were to be opened to the north and west of the old settlements. Other citizens at the time of the war held headright certificates that needed to be satisfied. Surveying was initiated and new counties designated. The frontier was being pushed farther westward and into Indian country.

A depressed land market had developed with the continuing policy of the infant Texas Republic in making land grants to new settlers, and the awarding of bounty lands for veterans. Veterans were unloading their 640-acre bounties for as little as 12 cents per acre. The Republic then fell back on printing of its own paper money, which further depressed the economy. Within a year Texas dollars had depreciated to 65 cents on the U.S. dollar. It soon dropped to two-for-one.

Scarcely had the noise of battle at San Jacinto died away and the ink dried on Texas Declaration of Independence than the call for opening of lands to the west began. The expansion to new lands would bring a long siege of death on the Plains of Texas for decades to come. The area of interest now was in the Tehuacana valley of Robertson's Colony, from the Brazos River eastward to the edge of the piney woods in East Texas.

The first settlers in the area came in 1835, moving up the Navasota River into what would become Limestone County. A colony of about 30 people including the Parker, Anglin, Frost, Bates, Plummer and Nixon families settled in an area which would be called Fort Parker. This was the extreme north edge of white settlement in the area, some 60 miles north of the Austin colony.

Elder John Parker, the leader of the group, was a hard-shell Baptist preacher out of Virginia, by way of Tennessee and Missouri. They found open, beautiful rich country, alive with wild game, including bear and deer. They built their cabins there, with a log stockade all around to protect them from the Indians known to traverse the land called the Comanche Trace. The following spring they broke the land and planted their crops. On the morning of May 19, 1836, most of the men returned to the fields to work, and were out of sight of the stockade. Six men and the women and children were left behind the walls.

Shortly after the noon meal, a band of Comanches and Kiowas approached the fort showing a dirty white flag and asking for water and a beef. Benjamin Parker parleyed with the braves outside the compound but told his brother, Silas, he felt the Indians were hostile. Parker told the Indians they had no beeves, and they became angry and pierced Parker with their lances. Silas ran for the fort but was cut down in his tracks. Two men named Frost were killed at the gates. Then, shrieking wildly, the Indians poured inside the fort.

Elder John Parker and Granny tried to run, but the Indians overtook them. They stabbed John Parker, scalped him and then cut off his private parts. Granny Parker was thrown to the ground, stripped and raped while a lance was held at her throat. The shouts from the fort brought the settlers on the run from the fields with their rifles in hand. Seeing the armed men arriving, the Indians mounted their horses and galloped off into the nearby woods of the Navasota River. Five dead men were left behind, along with several badly wounded women, two of who would later die. Granny Parker had been speared but pulled the lance out of her flesh and lived.

The Indians also took five captives: Rachael Plummer and her small son; Elizabeth Kellogg; and John and Cynthia Ann Parker, aged six and nine. The Comanches then rode northeast toward the Trinity River, where they stopped to hold a victory dance, then split up and vanished across the Red River and into Indian Territory. Rachael Plummer lived as a Comanche slave for eighteen months. She was finally sold to a Comanchero band, where she bore a child, but the Indians killed it in a cruel fashion because of its incessant crying during an illness. She was finally returned to Texas, where she soon died.

Elizabeth Kellogg was more fortunate. She fell into the hands of Caddoan allies of the Plains tribes, who took her to the Red River and sold her to a band of Delawares. The Delawares then sold her back to General Sam Houston in December, 1836, for $150. John Parker and James Plummer were found and ransomed in 1842. Young Parker, raised for six years as a Comanche, was never able to readjust to the pioneer life. He went back to the tribes looking for his sister. He finally married a Mexican girl who had been a Comanche slave and settled in Mexico.

Cynthia Ann Parker matured as a Comanche captive, and became the wife of Peta Nocona, war chief of the Comanches.

Cynthia Ann was the mother of Quanah Parker, who would lead the Comanches on a bloody warpath in Texas for four more decades. This violent, yet heart-rending story is well documented in Texas history.

In the summer of 1838, a surveying party, led by a Captain Neill, encountered a mixed band of Kickapoos, Kiowas and Comanches who were encamped in the vicinity killing buffalo. Objecting to the presence of the white intruders, the Indians attacked the party, killing seventeen of the twenty-three. This area in the Tehuacana watershed has since become known as Battle Creek. Word of the disaster reached some settlers at Franklin, and a party was organized to go to the scene and bury the dead. On the way to Battle Creek, the burial party chanced upon a survivor of the massacre, a Mr. Violet, at Tehuacana Springs, some 30 miles below the scene of the attack. Violet had been severely wounded and had been without food or water for six days. He had crawled on his hands and knees over rocks and through brush. He was near death when found by the party, but was taken back to Franklin where he was nursed back to health and lived to tell the tale.

The party continued their journey to the battleground, collecting and burying the remains of the seventeen victims of the savage and bloody battle. Descendants in later years erected a marble monument, on which is carved the names of the dead, and the survivors of the episode. The monument, behind a wrought-iron picket fence, is located one-mile west of present town of Dawson, on State Highway 31.

For a time the Tehuacana area returned to a state of peaceful serenity. The violent and bloody Indian encounters discouraged settlement in the area, but it was short lived. The need for more land and the desire of the Republic to settle more families gradually pushed the Indian frontier farther to the north and west. But the Indians and the settlers would continue to have problems for 40 more years.

Meanwhile, on Doe Run Creek, Andrew Miller continued his efforts to develop the plantation. His family was growing and he would need land for the future generations. Under the terms of his admission as a colonist he was entitled to a league and a labor of land. The Mexican government had granted the league of land on Doe Run Creek. He had received title February 26, 1831. He had never made application for his labor of land, 177 acres, that would be set aside for farming purposes. Miller went before the Washington County Board of Land Commissioners January 10, 1838 requesting assignment of his labor of land.

The commissioners approved the application, noting that Miller had arrived in Texas in 1824, was resident citizen at the time of Independence, and had remained a citizen ever since. All land in Washington County had been assigned, so it was necessary to search elsewhere. Open land was found in Brazos County, some 30 miles north of Miller's Doe Run league. After surveying by Adolphus Hope, the tract was approved and Certificate No. 31 assigned to Miller February 1, 1838. The land, located on Peach Creek near present College Station, Texas still bears the A. Miller survey designation, as does the Miller League in Washington County.

In March, Andrew Miller set out with his friend, Efrim Roddy, to travel to Brazos County to inspect land they had been assigned. The two men arrived at Miller's land first. Roddy left Miller to go to his own land, which was, located only two miles from the Miller survey. Roddy would return to Miller's land later in the afternoon and the two would make the return trip to Washington County. When he returned Roddy could not find Miller. He noted possible Indian signs, and places in the soil that appeared to be the scene of a skirmish. A further search of the land indicated horses had moved west. He followed a short way, but decided he should head home and report Miller missing.

Joseph Penn Lynch organized a search party. The party, including young Robert T. Miller, 16, set out to follow the tracks. The trail led west for a couple of miles, then turned north, following the Brazos River. Lynch was one of the first members of the ranging companies, which had been organized to deal with the

Indian problem to the settlers. He had made many forays into the wilderness and had much experience, but the party lost the trail.

Three days later, another group of Rangers encountered a band of Kiowas driving a string of stolen horses near present Caldwell. In the skirmish that followed, the Rangers killed two of the Kiowas and recovered all the horses. Six Kiowas escaped, making their way northwest. Miller's horse was among the stolen herd recovered by the Rangers, but his body was never found.

Andrew Miller's widow Celia, and Jos. P. Lynch was named administrators of the Andrew Miller estate in the May, 1838 term of court. Probate Judge Jno. P. Coles appointed Miller's good friends, John Lott and E. Roddy to submit an inventory and appraisal of the estate. The list of real and personal property submitted June 25, 1838, showed a value of $29,656. Assets included 2,298 acres of land on Doe Run Creek, and 1,036 acres of land lying on Caney Creek. The inventory listed 11slaves by first name; five horses; four yoke of oxen; 27 head of cattle and 10 head of hogs, plus items of personal property. Heirs to the estate were Celia; Mary Miller Lynch, 18; Robert T., 16; Merideth Neal, 10, and Lucretia, seven.

Unpaid bills charged by Miller before his death was submitted to the estate for payment. According to some of the purchases by Miller, boy's shoes sold for $1.50 per pair; Rum and brandy was 25 cents per half pint; whiskey was $1.25 gallon; ribbon, 25 cents per yard; women's shoes, $2.50 per pair; candle moulds, $1.00 per pair; and nails, 35 per pound.

A runaway slave belonging to the Miller estate, a man named Loyd, was causing some problems after Miller's death. Bills submitted to the estate included a charge from Wm. G. Evans of Houston, on July 29, 1838, for "examining a Negro man belonging to the Andrew Miller estate, and committing him to jail." The charge for the service was two dollars.

Sheriff J.W. Moon, of Houston, submitted a bill to the estate in the amount of four dollars, for two commitments and two releases of a Negro man, Loyd. The receipt from the sheriff noted that Jos.

P. Lynch had paid the bill in "Texas money," two dollars for one dollar, for a total of eight dollars.

Another statement received was from Dr. William P.

Smith, of Washington, in the amount of $25.00 for "medical services rendered the Negroes of the Andrew Miller estate for the year 1838." Andrew Lawson, of Houston, submitted a bill in the amount of $46.50 for "boarding a Negro man from July 29 to August 28, 1838," at $1.50 per day. This was probably the runaway Loyd, since the dates coincide with the time Loyd was jailed in Houston by the sheriff.

Celia Miller and Lynch had petitioned the court for permission to sell Loyd during the June, 1838 term. The petition stated: "There are debts owing by said estate, and there is a Negro man named Loyd belonging to said estate which your petitioners think in the best interest to sell, both on account of the debts owing, and the difficulty in managing said Negro man in the family." Judge Coles approved the petition June 25, 1838.

R.B. Peck, of Washington, is shown as the purchaser of the Negro man, Loyd, for $1,000 in "Texas money." Peck also purchased a pony from the estate in the amount of $100, "paid in good money," as noted in estate documents.

John Lott and Celia Miller were married at Washington, March 12, 1839. Lott had become a widower at the time, and had one daughter, Louisa, age 11, still at home. One of Lott's other daughters, Sarah Ann, had married James R. Cook December 19, 1837. Cook was the San Jacinto hero who, having purchased a horse for $25 from Lott, had the animal run away with him behind the Mexican lines prior to the main battle. Celia had been appointed guardian of the three Miller children who had not yet reached majority. The merged families lived for a time on the Miller survey, but soon moved to Grimes County, across the Navasota River, where Lott had a plantation.

James Cook and Sarah Ann were deeded some 665 acres of the Andrew Miller survey on Doe Run Creek by John Lott. In executing the deed, Lott noted the deed was "in and for the natural love and affection which I bear to my daughter, Sarah Ann Cook and my son-in-law, James R. Cook." Cook was a planter and a horse breeder. He set about building a racetrack on Doe Run, and the track was the scene of many spirited races.

Cook was particularly fond of a blooded race horse he called "Monseiur Towson." On March 31, 1843, Cook and a friend, a man named Adkins, were having some drinks at a Washington bar when Adkins made an apparent derogatory remark about Cook's favorite horse. Cook took umbrage to the remark, and returned a comment, whereupon Adkins struck Cook with a riding whip. The enraged Cook pulled the Bowie knife he always carried in his belt, and began stabbing Adkins. Adkins finally was able to pull a pistol, and shot Cook dead. Adkins had been stabbed 14 times, but survived the altercation. Cook was only 30 years old at the time of the "affray," as the newspaper reported the incident. Cook was buried at Farquhar Cemetery, not far from their plantation on Doe Run Creek.

Following Cook's death, Sarah leased their home to Dr. Anson Jones while his plantation, Barrington, was being constructed nearby. Jones was the last Governor of the Republic of Texas. Sarah married a surveyor, Hartwell C. Fountain, and they moved to Seguin, in Guadalupe County. Cook's beloved sorrel horse was sold to Sarah's uncle, Robert A. Lott, for the sum of $140.00.

The Austin colonist, Andrew Miller, was now dead. John Lott and Celia had married, taking the remaining children with them to a new home in Grimes County. Jos. P. Lynch had been noticing beautiful, new country to the northwest during his pursuit of Indians during his term of service with the ranging companies. He had particular interest in land on Tehuacana Creek, near the village of Waco Indians.

Life for the families was about to change.

Lost Grave of Texas Hero Found By Pam Puryear

At right: Pamela Puryear with rescued headstone of J.R. Cook

Pamela Ashworth Puryear (1943–2005) was a great-grand daughter of Robert A. Lott who operated a hotel at Washington-On-The-Brazos in the colonial and Republic era of early Texas. Obtaining a Masters Degree from Texas A&M College, she became an authority on the Victorian clothing of women in the period, and authored three books on history of the area, including "Sternwheelers and Sandbars," a history of travel and commerce on the Barazos River.

An original founder of the "Texas Rose Rustlers," she traveled the Austin Colony area seeking vintage roses the early settlers planted on homesteads and cemeteries. She would take cuttings from the roses and share with others and nurseries in propagating the roses. "Pam's Pink," and Climbing Pamela," varieties are named in her honor.

It was on a mission of rescuing vintage roses that Pamela discovered the long-forgotten grave of Col. James R. Cook in Farquhar Cemetery just north of Old Washington. Cook, a hero of battles at San Antonio de Bexar and at San Jacinto. Cook's grave was covered with underbrush and briar thickets that were practically impenetrable. Cook's headstone was cleaned, reset by stonemasons.

An Inventory and appraisment of the real and personal property belonging to the succession of Andrew Miller Dec.ᵈ

2298. Acres of land lying near the Towng of Washington @ 8.$/ per Acre $18384

1036. Acres of land lying on Camp Creek @ 4.$/ per Acre . . . . . . $ 4 11.

Negro man Washington	1 1.5.4.
Negro man Loyd	600.
Negro Woman Maria	800.
Negro Woman Delphia	460.
Negro Boy Nathan	800
Negro Girl Casline	500.
Negro Girl Matilda	400.
Negro Girl Rachel	350.
Negro Girl Nancy	360.
Negro Boy Alfred	360
Negro Boy William	250.
One read Waggon	180
One Grey horse	180.
One Grey horse	80.
One Bay horse	80.
One Grey filley	125
One Brown Mare	50.
Sone Yokes of Oxen @ 80.$/ per Yoke	320.
Seventeen Cows & Calves @ 20$/ per Cow & Calf	340
Four two year old Cattle @ 10$/ per head	40.
Eight Yearling Cattle @ 7.$/ per head	56.
Ten head of Stock hogs	30
Three Ox Yokes @ 5.$/ per Yoke	15
Three Ox Chains @ 5$/ per Chain	15
One Nelse of hand on R. B. Rech. for	160.
Aggregate . . . . $	29,656.

Page one, appraisal, Andrew Miller estate.

Republic of Texas.
Washington County. Personally appeared John Lott and
E. Roddy in Open Court and made Oath that, in Obedience
to an Order of this Court they have proceeded to make an
Inventory and an appraisment of the property both real and
personal, belonging to the Succession of Andrew Miller dec'd.
and that the foregoing Schedule Contains a true, and honest
and correct [illegible] Administrator
of said Succession.
    Sworn to, and Subscribed, in Open Court this [illegible] day
    of June 1838.

J no. P. Coles   _John Lott_
Judge of Probate   _E. Roddy_

Republic of Texas
Washington County [illegible] approved
[illegible] [illegible] to Record 25 June 1838

                              J no. P. Coles
                              Judge of Probate

From Andrew Miller probate file

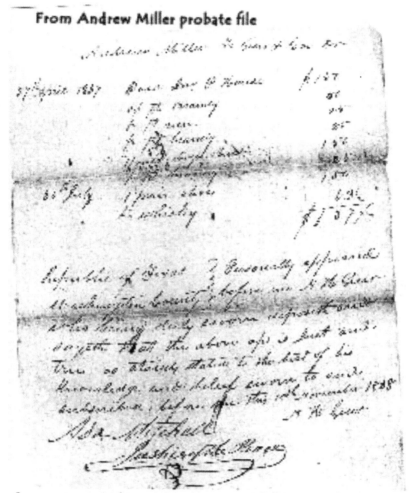

The items purchased by Andrew Miller in his account with Greer and Coe shows his home was stocked with brandy, rum and whiskey in 1837. Two pairs of shoes were purchased at $1.50 per pair.

RELOCATING TO THE TEHUACANA VALLEY

Joseph Penn Lynch was 21 years of age when he came to Texas from Kentucky in 1831. He had received an excellent education, and had even read some law. He was slight of stature, but his jet-black hair and flashing dark eyes commanded attention wherever he went. The personable Lynch settled in the town of Washington-on-the-Brazos where he was initially engaged as a tutor. There were no schools in the Austin colony at the time, so it was necessary to receive private instruction. One of Lynch's students was Mary Miller, Andrew and Celia Miller's first born, whom he would later marry.

Lynch took an early, active role in the affairs of Washington and the colony. He was elected as a chief judicial officer (called an Alcalde in Spanish Texas), for the town of Washington. He was also an early volunteer in the Ranging Company of Capt. Philip Coe, being mustered July 9, 1835. The principal objective of the ranging companies was to protect the settlements against Indian attacks. From

Joseph Penn Lynch

these early ranging companies would later be born the famous Texas Rangers. Lynch regularly went on searching missions in the frontier as a ranger to recover stolen livestock and engage the Indians whenever they were found.

Sterling Clack Robertson had been granted an empresario

contract by the Mexican legislature on April 29, 1834. Like Austin, the object of his contract was to locate homesteaders in the vast area of central Texas assigned to him. Robertson's grant stretched out of Washington County from the Brazos and Colorado Rivers on the east and west, to several hundred miles north to the area of present Dallas.

Robertson's colony had been besieged with lawsuits and Indian depredations from the start. Austin had purposely selected an area where he believed Indian problems would be at a minimum. The events would prove it was a correct decision. But as settlers began moving north and west out of Austin's colony and into Robertson's district the problems with Indians became more acute. They began facing the plains tribes who were fiercer in defense against the white intrusion.

Robertson had come to Texas from Tennessee. His father, James Robertson, had founded the city of Nashville in 1780, so the young Robertson had experience in land development. He established a colonial capital at Viesca, near the falls of the Brazos River. In October 1835, the town of Viesca sent a delegation to the Consultation at San Felipe de Austin. On December 25 the Consultation changed the name to Milam, as a memorial to Benjamin Milam, who had been killed in the capture of San Antonio de Bexar. Robertson made his home near the falls and became well acquainted with the Captain through Lynch's duties as sheriff and as a ranger.

Lynch had gone with Coe's ranging company to the northern reaches of Robertson's colony shortly after his muster in July 1835. Coe's company was sent to dislodge a band of Tawakoni Indians at Tehuacana Springs, in present Limestone County, but on arrival they discovered the Indians had fled. He had participated in other sorties in the new territory and had become familiar with the area.

The participation of Lynch in the storming and capture of San Antonio de Bexar, the battle for Independence at San Jacinto, and his service in the ranging companies had resulted in Lynch receiving many bounties of land in several areas of Texas. He maintained residence at Washington after he and Mary Miller were married, but he was still widely traveled in Texas frontier areas. Lynch had made many excursions into the Robertson colony, where settlers in the outpost areas were susceptible to attack by the plains tribes of Comanche and Kiowa Indians.

Lynch was particularly impressed with the area along the Brazos River in the Robertson colony. A small fort had been built in 1837 by the ranging companies on the banks of the Brazos River, near the site of an ancient settlement of Waco Indians. The fort was named Fort Fisher. A settlement of Wacos still existed there, but the fort was soon abandoned because its location was so remote and vulnerable to pillage when not manned by the rangers.

Stephen F. Austin had sent Capt. A.C. Buckner and a party of men to the Waco Village in June 1824, to make a treaty with the tribes. Both parties had generally honored the treaty. The Wacos were basically a friendly people and rarely caused major troubles with the settlers. They maintained a trading relationship with the plains tribes, but were not nomadic as were their Plains Indian cousins.

The tribe was of a Wichita culture, and their village on the Brazos consisted of sixty to seventy conical, bee-hive shaped dwellings, about twenty-five feet high, thatched with willow and grass. The settlement was permanent, occupying some four hundred acres on which they raised corn, beans, pumpkins and melons. Their diet also consisted of the various selections of wild game, including buffalo. The land in these northern reaches of the Robertson colony frontier was rich and fertile. Lynch had even received some land bounty in the region with an eye for future development.

Following the death of Andrew Miller and the subsequent marriage of Celia Miller to John Lott, the family structure changed. In a short time the family moved across the Brazos to John Lott's plantation in Grimes County. John and Celia Lott were both substantial land owners and they engaged in buying and selling real estate.

Shortly after the revolution, John Lott sold his interest in the Lott & Hall operation to his partner, Jack Hall. He was now active in real estate, but maintained an interest in his plantation, as well as that of the Miller family, which was now being supervised by Lott, Celia and young Robert Miller. Under their supervision the improvements on the Doe Run and Caney Creek plantations of the Miller estate had increased substantially.

The first addition to the Jos. P. Lynch family occurred with the birth of William Andrew July 16, 1838. Then followed the births of Joseph Milam, June 24, 1840; Mary Etta, July 5, 1841; Annie Eliza, January 4, 1843 and Laura Cecelia, June 15, 1847.

Lynch maintained his political leadership posture, and was elected Sheriff of Washington County February 1, 1841. He defeated Elijah Sterling Clack Robertson, the son of the empresario, by the slim margin of 13 votes. One of his duties was to act as a tax collector, which was necessary now in the new republic. He set about his new duties vigorously, and provided much needed governmental revenues while keeping the peace. Sporadic Indian activity in the area also had to be met in his duties as sheriff and ranger.

There was still concern about the Indian problem on the frontier. Settlers on the fringes of the new settlements were repeatedly attacked by roving bands of Comanche and Kiowas. The hero of San Jacinto, Sam Houston, was now president of the Republic of Texas, and the Indian problem drew his attention.

At Houston's urging, Republic of Texas lawmakers on January 14, 1843, had authorized the establishment of Indian trading posts. A stockholder group organized by the Torrey Brothers of Asford, Connecticut, had established the first post at New Braunfels. Houston requested one of the brothers, Thomas S. Torrey, to journey to the Waco Village in Robertson's colony, and establish a second trading post. Torrey set out with a partner, George Barnard, in March 1843, and they selected a spot on Tehuacana Creek, some eight miles below the village as its location.

The following September, Houston called for a meeting

Jesse Chisholm

between Texas officials and the Indian representatives in an effort to effect a peaceful solution to the problems. He called on his old friend from the Indian Territory days, Jesse Chisholm, to attend and direct activities of the effort. Chisholm was known and respected by the Indians, particularly the Comanches, with whom Houston hoped to reach a peaceful coexistence.

Chisholm had journeyed from his home in Indian Territory, and was in attendance at the meeting on the Tehuacana Creek, near Torrey's Trading Post. Also attending was Thomas Torrey, whom Houston had appointed as Indian Agent for the region. A group of Wacos, Caddoes and lesser tribes attended, but the Comanches did not. The meeting, called the Tehuacana Creek Council, resulted in a treaty, but meant little with the absence of the most feared and influential tribe in Texas--the Comanche. Several other councils were called at the location, but none were successful in attracting any important Comanche representatives. The last council ended November 16, 1845, again without any important Comanche in attendance.

Torrey's Trading Post remained an important frontier installation despite the death of Thomas Torrey on a return trip to the Texas interior. He was taken ill as he traveled along the Brazos, and died on September 28, 1843. His partner, George Barnard, continued the operation, opening branch posts on the Navasota River, and near the falls of the Brazos, some 30 miles below Waco. Barnard, a 26 year old native of Connecticut, resided at the post, and was the first white settler in the Waco region.

The layout of the trading post consisted of seven log houses built out of rough, unhewn logs. The post did not contain any protective outer walls. The safety of the post, it was said, was founded on its usefulness and necessity to the Indian. The largest of the log houses contained the pelts received from the Indians. Some were brought in entirely raw, or green, and tanned at the post before shipment. Most pelts were scraped by hand and tanned, and some even decorated by the Indians.

Aside from the skins, mules were an especially important trade item, with Comanches bringing in mules captured from the northern provinces of Mexico. Most were unbroken and totally wild, but when gentled would bring $40 each. The Rangers usually bought the mules to be used as pack animals.

Some of the log houses served as living quarters for various persons who resided there. One resident was an Indian agent. Another was a gunsmith. The Indians usually came in numbers, riding single file, the men riding ahead, the women riding behind, with a papoose or two riding in a saddle with her. Packhorses carried the hides and household goods. The hides were brought to the warehouse, weighed, and a value determined. The Indians then selected goods equivalent to the price agreed to. A visit by the Indians usually lasted several days with them camped out around the trading post.

Under the management of Barnard the trading post became highly successful, attracting Indians from all tribes from hundreds of miles away. Merchandise was mostly bartered, with the Indians bringing in pelts of all descriptions to trade for gun powder, lead, bullet molds, hatchets, colored beads, blankets, cloth, combs and tobacco. Deer hides were the biggest item of barter. Buffalo robes were also plentiful. Barnard's well-kept books recorded the handling of 75,000 hides between 1844 and 1853. The hides were sorted, packed in bales, and freighted to Houston by ox wagon. There they were sent to the eastern United States where buffalo robes were highly popular as wagon and sleigh blankets.

In 1848, Barnard bought out the remaining Torrey Brothers for $9,500. When the town of Waco was laid out in 1849 at the Waco Indian Spring, Barnard bought lot 1, block 1, and moved his stock from the trading post on the Tehuacana. The old post buildings stood for many years, the last being destroyed by fire in 1929.

Receiving a One-Third League land bounty on Tehuacana Creek, February 20, 1838, was Revolution veteran Francisco Garza. The deed, File No. 6, Robertson County First Class, was deeded to Garza, and signed by Republic President Sam Houston himself. Garza appeared before the Washington County Land Commissioners, with the board quickly granting approval.

The board noted that Garza had arrived in Texas in 1833, was a single man, a native Mexican, but had served with the Texian army, and was wounded. Garza, just two days after acquiring the land, sold his land bounty to Washington lawyer, William W. Arrington, for the sum of two hundred dollars.

Robertson's Colony covered a vast area of central Texas, and was known as Robertson County. In 1845 Limestone County was created out of this district because of the great distance to the capital at Franklin. The area attracted the attention of the Jos. P. Lynch, the Lott and Miller and families and they began purchasing land in Limestone County.

Jos. P. Lynch purchased the Garza survey land on Tehuacana Creek from Arrington in January 1846. He then sold almost 700 acres of the property to Robert T. Miller, and kept nearly 1,000 acres in his own name. The land was only a few miles north of the Torrey Trading Post. The soil was rich and fertile. It would make an excellent homestead location for Miller.

John and Celia Lott bought land in Limestone County, near the newly designated town of Springfield, which would become the county seat. The town was created by the legislature in April 1846. Elisha Anglin and George Calmes were appointed to plat the township of Springfield, which would cover 500 acres.

Springfield was located on the Navasota River, just two miles south of Fort Parker, where the massacre and capture of the Parker clan had occurred just ten years before. Another attempt had been made to settle the country after the Fort Parker incident, but the residents again were forced to flee. The country was still occupied by unfriendly Indians, and the prairies contained a population of panthers and bears. This time the country was gaining population and settlement attempts would be better accomplished.

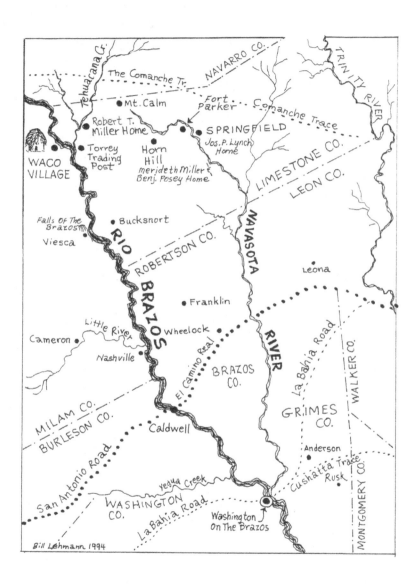

FAMILY DEATHS AND THE CIVIL WAR

Following the purchase of the Garza survey lands by Robert T. Miller in February 1846 from his brother-in-law, Miller began building his new homestead. He became one of the first settlers on the Tehuacana. Miller brought to the homestead location a wagonload of supplies to begin building the needed homes. He also brought with him two male slaves, and the trio set about building two houses: one for Miller, and the other for the slaves that came with him to the new home. Miller was still single, but he and John Lott's youngest daughter, Louisa, would soon be married, and would occupy the home when completed.

On January 4, 1839, the Texas Legislature had passed a land provision law granting lands to new settlers. Its purpose was to entice new immigrants, thereby increasing the population sufficiently to insure acceptance of Texas into the Union as a new state. Robert Miller, though a citizen of Texas since 1824, qualified for an allotment of 320 acres under the provision of the law. His application was approved December 23, 1839.

Miller had selected four parcels of land and called for a survey on each. After surveying, it was discovered each parcel encroached on the boundaries of land already assigned others, causing a delay in his anticipated move from Washington. He then purchased the Garza survey land from Lynch until his land allotment could be successfully surveyed.

Robert Miller and the two slaves began felling trees with which to erect the houses. The main house was of the typical dog-trot construction, a cabin on each end, with a common roof extended over both. A fireplace was built on each cabin to stave off the winter chill. The slave quarters were a single cabin with a fireplace. A central, smaller cabin was located near the main house where meals were cooked, clothes washed, meat butchered, processed, salted and smoked. The food at tables of both families was the same: Corn and pork, and pork and corn.

Sawmills now made lumber available, and Miller brought

lumber for flooring of the cabins. Windows contained no glass. Slots were sawed out of the logs and fitted with rough sliding panels. On mild days, muslin cloth was hung over the window openings to permit light to enter the rooms. Water would come from nearby Tehuacana Creek, where it was abundant even in dry periods. Wild game was plentiful, as were native pecans, walnuts, berries and wild greens.

Robert Miller, 25, and Louisa Lott, 19, were married in the spring of 1847, and she came to live in the house he had prepared on the Tehuacana. Robert's inheritance from the Andrew Miller estate included a slave family, which also lived near their house in their own quarters. The first crops of corn and cotton were planted. The work was hard and there were no luxuries on the frontier.

The Miller homestead was near the Torrey Trading Post, where they were constantly aware of Indian presence. Each time they glanced up from their chores they would see Indians on the horizon, traveling single file, on their way to the trading post. They prayed the peace treaties would permit them a peaceful existence in their new home on the Texas prairie. None of the frontier settlers in early Texas would be accused of being faint-of-heart. The Miller's were no exception.

The Texas landscape in spring brought a glowing description from a German writer, Frederick Roemer, who traveled through the area in 1847: "There is no spectacle more fascinating than the prairie of Texas during the months of April, May and June. They spread themselves out before him like a costly carpet, richly green, with embroidery of exquisite flowers of diverse colors. One cannot help but be apprehensive that the hoof of the horse does not trample these marvels of nature and disarrange their harmony," Roemer wrote in his journal.

John and Celia Lott continued their pursuit of Texas real estate interests, buying and selling large numbers of parcels. Lott's plantation home in Grimes County now numbered only three since Louisa had married Robert Miller. Merideth Neal Miller had been sent to Alexandria, Louisiana, to live with Celia's Neal relatives while he attended school. Lucretia was 14, and was being tutored.

Jos. P. Lynch moved his family from Washington to the Limestone County capital town of Springfield in 1847. There he became active in politics, real estate, merchandising, and civic affairs. Springfield was growing. A road out of Houston now passed through Washington up to Springfield. The road then branched out to Palestine and Fairfield to the east. A road to the west, connecting Waco was becoming more widely traveled.

Lynch established a general merchandise store in Springfield. Numerous friendly Indians now inhabited the area, some trading with Lynch. On one occasion the store was crowded with Indians, one of which was a new mother who had a baby wrapped in a blanket. Lynch took the bundle and went to his house to show the baby to Mary and the children. The Indians, not knowing his intent, became very excited and followed him. They soon realized no harm would come to the child when they saw the Lynch family doting over the infant. Satisfied, the Indians then returned to the store, and Lynch soon returned the infant to its mother.

Texas attained statehood in 1846, and there was jubilation. It had taken a full ten years following the Revolution, and Texans now breathed a little easier with air from the United States settling over the new state. A temporary capital had been located at Washington-on-the-Brazos during the Revolution. It had since been moved to Austin, on the Colorado River. Many people were not happy with the Austin location. With statehood status, a permanent capital would now be selected. Lynch was one of the Springfield citizens who parleyed to locate the state capital there. The move was not successful, but it was a valiant effort on behalf of the citizens in the fledgling community.

The first tax roll for Limestone County was completed February 16, 1847. 213 names appeared on the first landowner tax rolls, including Robert T. Miller, Celia Lott and John Lott. By 1848, the town of Springfield counted 120 inhabitants. The town was incorporated March 1, 1848.

The first U.S. federal census of 1850 for Limestone County showed a population of 2,608. Negro slaves numbered 618. There were 882 white females, and 1,108 white males were counted. Springfield now sported a new 20 x 30 foot wooden building in which to conduct county business and hold county records.

Returning to Texas from his studies in Louisiana was Merideth Miller. He soon found land northwest of Springfield, on Horn Hill, where he established a stock-raising venture. Horn Hill was originally called Mount Vernon. It has the highest elevation in the area, offering a wide view of the countryside.

Lucretia Miller had come to live with the Lynch family in Springfield. Mary was in poor health, and Lucretia would be of great help to the family even though Mary had a house servant. A son, Nathaniel Lynch, had been born January 1, 1849, but he died March 10, 1849. His grave in the Springfield cemetery is the oldest recorded grave there.

Another daughter would be born to the Lynches with the arrival of Lucretia Penn Lynch, January 24, 1851. The children now numbered six. Lucretia Miller, Mary's younger sister, left the household in September 1850. She married Franklin C. Oliver, who had come to Texas with his family from Tennessee.

Mary's health continued to deteriorate and she died June 12, 1852 following a lengthy and painful illness. Her mother, Celia Lott, was among those at her bedside at the time of death. She was buried next to her infant son, Nathaniel, in the Springfield cemetery. Mary Miller Lynch was only 32 years of age at the time of her death.

The Jos. P. Lynch family was saddened with the death of their wife and mother. For unknown reasons the children of Joseph and Mary took residence with separate family members in other locations. The two oldest boys, William Andrew and Joseph Milam, went to live with friends in western Limestone County. Two of the Lynch daughters, Mary Etta and Lucretia Penn, went to the home of Frank and Lucretia Oliver in Springfield. The two other daughters, Annie Eliza and Laura Cecelia, went to live with

Neal relatives in Rapides Parish, Louisiana, near Alexandria.

Lynch himself remarried Sarah Jane Nalley in 1857. The marriage was short lived as they had already divorced when a daughter, Blache Lynch was born in July 1859. Joseph P. Lynch is shown living in the Springfield household of Washington S Wallace in the 1860 U.S. census for McLennan County. It is believed that Wallace's wife, Margaret, was Lynch's sister. Sarah and Blanche are shown living in the household of her uncle, Virgil Nalley in the 1860 census.

Lynch is said to have died in 1861, but it is not known where he died or is buried. The Springfield cemetery records do not show him buried there. The Texas Historical Commission placed a large 3 x 6 ft, granite marker at the graves of Mary and Nathaniel Lynch. It was placed there in 1976 on the 150th anniversary of Texas' Independence to honor veterans of the Revolution. A courthouse fire in 1874 destroyed all official records for Limestone County including marriage and divorce records. The old Springfield cemetery is now a part of Fort Parker State Park, located three miles east of Groesbeck.

Meanwhile, the Robert Miller homestead on Tehuacana Creek was now a part of newly created McLennan County. In the fall of 1850, the Limestone County boundary had been pushed back east about fifteen miles to create the new adjoining McLennan County. Waco was designated as the county seat. The Miller household had increased with the birth of two daughters. Celia Frances was born in July 1850. She was named for Robert's mother. Another daughter, Sarah Ann, arrived March 22, 1852. Sarah was named for the mother and sister of Louisa.

The family had not been without problems. The head of the slave family, Johnathan, had died of an epidemic that struck in 1851. He left a wife and two small children. Miller then acquired another male slave from Joseph P. Lynch to assist him. A new slave cabin had been constructed for his new helper.

Two bountiful cotton crops had been produced and sent to Houston, but two other cotton crops had been meager due to a wet planting season in one, and a drought during the growing season in the next. The production, though somewhat curtailed, had still resulted in some needed cash revenues to the household however. The corn crops had been adequate to feed the family and the livestock. The numbers of horses, cattle and hogs had increased, and the family did not want for food. The Torrey Trading Post had been relocated to Waco, but the Miller family still eyed with apprehension the passing of Indians by the homestead.

The death of Mary Lynch in 1852 was followed by the horrible death of John Lott in the same year. Lott had been surprised by a small band of Kiowa Indians at Kellum Springs, in Grimes County. Lott attempted to flee to safety of a neighboring homestead, but his horse fell after stepping in a hole, spilling him on the ground. The Indians showed no mercy to their white captive. Lott was speared with lances, scalped, stripped naked, and his body horribly mutilated. A searching party organized by neighbors lost the trail of the Indians, and they disappeared in the wilderness.

After first settling at Horn Hill, Merideth Miller then moved to Honest Ridge, just a few miles north of Horn Hill. Honest Ridge was a beautiful area, on top of a ridge that permitted visibility of the countryside for miles around. He married Lucy Eller Oliver March 14, 1854. Lucy was the sister of Franklin C. Oliver, who had married Merideth's sister, Lucretia Miller. Merideth and Frank Oliver both would become merchants at Groesbeck in addition to being stock raisers.

The Robert Miller family was the next to feel the horrors of death at the hands of Indians. Robert and his slave, Jim, were searching the brushy bottoms of Tehuacana Creek for some stray yearlings when they were surprised by a small band of seven Indians passing through the area. Miller had dismounted and advanced up the creek. Jim was searching another nearby area when he heard a skirmish in the brush.

Miller had left his rifle with the horse, but was carrying his pistol with him. The Indians surprised Miller and went on the attack. The shrill cry of the Indian attack alerted Jim to the impending danger. He went to Miller's horse, retrieved the rifle, and was advancing toward the noise when he heard the discharge of Miller's pistol. The return fire of an Indian with a rifle struck Miller in the left shoulder, spinning him around. He readied his aim for the next round when an arrow struck him in the heart, killing him instantly. Jim arrived on the scene and delivered a shot from Miller's rifle at an Indian across the creek. He had time to see his bullet hit its mark, severely wounding the Indian that had been his target. But Jim caught an arrow in the shoulder from another Indian, which disabled him.

As the Indians were advancing on Jim to deliver a final blow, he heard shouts coming from the rear. A group of neighbors from the area had gathered for a weekend prayer meeting when they heard the shouts of the Indians and the gunfire. The men were constructing a brush arbor at the meeting site, but halted their activities to investigate the noise. Spotting the approaching settlers, the Indians began to flee. The Indian Jim had wounded with the rifle was shot dead from his horse by a settler. The rescuers killed two others, but four escaped. The settlers identified the dead Indians as Kiowas.

Miller's body was buried the next day near a large oak tree. He was 31 years of age. A Baptist preacher, who had gathered the group for the brush arbor meeting, delivered last rites. Jim's wound was more serious than first believed. He died a painful death a few weeks later. He was buried near Miller, on the banks of Tehuacana Creek. Louisa was left with the two infants and three minor female slaves. Jim left no known family.

Louisa now was faced with keeping the homestead together. Help came at times from neighbors. Jos. P. Lynch sent another male slave to handle the heavy chores, plant the crops, and tend the livestock. Frank Oliver, Lucretia's husband, sent help during harvest and fall butchering. The slaves cared for Celia Frances and Sarah Ann Miller. Hamilton Cohron, a neighbor from nearby Mt. Calm, who had been in the rescuing party also offered help.

The Cohron family had come to Texas in 1849 from Georgia. The father, Isaac Cohron, had brought his wife, Rachael, and six children. Hamilton C. Cohron was the oldest of the children. He was born in 1820. The family settled at Mt. Calm, in the northwest part of Limestone County, where they farmed.

Hamilton Cohron began paying frequent visits to the Miller homestead after the tragedy, and romance soon developed. Cohron and Louisa were married in 1854, one year after Robert Miller's death. They continued to farm at the Tehuacana Creek homestead but intended to relocate to Mt. Calm as soon as a pending Settler's Claim was approved to Cohron.

Cohron's 160-acre Settler's Claim was approved August 11, 1859, and signed by Texas Governor H.R. Runnels. Its location was some three miles below Mt. Calm, and seven miles east of the Miller homestead on Tehuacana Creek. The Limestone County land maps still identify the property as the H.C. Cohron survey.

Following the approval of the Cohron Settler's Claim, Louisa had the Miller property on Tehuacana Creek divided, and she sold her half interest. The other half, some 333 acres, was held by the surviving daughters of the Miller estate, Celia Frances, and Sarah Ann Miller. The family then moved to the new homestead on Salt Creek, near Mt. Calm. Cohron and Louisa subsequently became the parents of three daughters: Elizabeth, born in 1855; Laura Jane, born September 25, 1858, and Ellen, born July 29, 1861.

Another event would affect the Garza survey land on Tehuacana Creek: Jos. P. Lynch had retained the nearly 1,000 acres of the property in his name at the time of purchase in 1846. Apparently ill, and feeling death was imminent, he began deeding all his real and personal property to his children.

In a document dated August 15, 1859, Lynch deeded "Because of the love and affection I hold for my two sons, William Andrew and Joseph M. Lynch, a one-half interest each in the Francisco Garza survey, at the fork of Tehuacana Creek." The deed also carried title to 100 head of horses; 800 head of cattle; a Negro woman named Gitty; her son, Wade, age three; a stallion; a jack, and three yoke of oxen. Similar deeds were conveyed to all his children covering his remaining property in several counties.

Arriving to Texas from North Carolina in 1859 was the family of Washington S. Wallace. Wallace and his wife, Margaret, settled at first near Springfield, but then relocated to the northern reaches of the Navasota River, near Mt. Calm sometime after 1860. Their six children consisted of Matthew Alexander; Mary Roxanna; Elizabeth; Sarah; William W., and Robert Wiley. All had been born in North Carolina. Wallace was a stock raiser and farmer. The family was counted in the 1860 census for the Springfield precinct.

The Horn Hill area of Limestone County would receive the Benjamin F. Posey family, from Alabama, via a short stay at Nacogdoches. Benjamin Posey and his wife, Eliza, were both one-half Creek Indians. They arrived at Horn Hill with 15 children, fourteen of which had been born in Alabama. The last child, Eliza Hulda, had been born in Nacogdoches in 1849. The family relocated to Limestone County sometime after 1850.

Horn Hill proved to be an ideal place for the Posey children to mature. Benjamin Posey was a stock raiser and had brought with him to Texas a breed stock of fine horses. The eight Posey sons had plenty of room to perfect their ranching skills. All were excellent horsemen. The youngest son, William Andrew Jackson Posey, was especially proficient as a judge of fine horseflesh, and he was an excellent trainer of horses. Texas would remember his name.

The Cohron, Wallace and Posey families all lived within a stone's throw of one another. The families attended church together, and the children were schooled together. In 1860 they began hearing rumblings about an issue that would divide the country and result in a war between the Northern and Southern states. The Civil War would have a profound effect on their lives.

With the Declaration of war, the men began enlisting in the Confederate Army. Merideth Miller, Frank C. Oliver, William Andrew Lynch, Joseph Milam Lynch, Washington Wallace, Benjamin Posey, Matthew A. Wallace and William A. Posey all mustered in for service with the Confederates. Their service would be mostly in Louisiana, Arkansas and Indian Territory.

The Lynch brothers enlisted at Springfield and were assigned to the Terry's Texas Rangers command. The unit fought in many of the famous battles. The Texans practiced a ritual of loud yells on entering the battles. This was soon recognized and credited with being the "Rebel Yell" of the Confederates. The young William Andrew Lynch was wounded twice in the same day in battles at Rome, Georgia. The wounds would plague him the rest of his life.

Tragedy would again strike Louisa when Hamilton C. Cohron died in 1865. He had contracted a fever in an epidemic that swept the country, and died within a few days after coming down with the illness. Louisa was again widowed, this time left with five minor children: two by Robert Miller, and three by Hamilton Cohron. Hamilton's brother, John Cohron, had recently returned from service in the Confederate army and moved in with his brother's family, handling the necessary farm chores.

With the surrender of Robert E. Lee at Appomattox, the conflict between the states was ended. The tired and weary sons of Texas began returning home to devastated and ruined farms. Little did the people of Texas and the South realize that Reconstruction would be worse than the war.

A.J. Burleson stated in his writings "there was sorrow on every hand. It was a sickening thing to see. All about us stalked the giant of poverty, hunger and disease. Our cattle had been scattered to the winds. We knew not where to find them. However, we were so glad the struggle had ended. We undertook our tasks in good humor and made the best of it."

The women the Texans left behind had matured. Even in the face of such poverty, romance soon blossomed and marriages began to happen. The first to marry was Bill Posey and Elizabeth Wallace, wed July 18, 1865. Then came Celia Frances Miller, who married Benjamin B. Lofland September 26, 1867. Lofland was a planter, but they set up a home in Springfield. Also marrying in 1867 was Joseph Milam Lynch and Mary Roxanna Wallace.

Louisa's third marriage also came in 1867, when she married

Albert A. Aikman, of Hill County. John Cohron, the brother of Hamilton, had met Aikman during the war. Aikman had come to help Cohron with the cotton harvest, and met Louisa. A courtship ensued and the two were soon married. Celia Frances Miller had married, but the household still held four minor children.

Albert A. Aikman was born in Tennessee in 1816, and came to Texas sometime after 1860, and was engaged in farming in southern Hill County at the time he married Louisa. He had got caught up in the Civil War, enlisting January 20, 1864, at Hillsboro for a term of six months. He served in Company G, First Cavalry Regiment, 2nd Brigade. He was 48 at the time of enlistment. Aikman and Louisa continued to farm the Cohron survey, but bought their own 80-acre farm in McLennan County on the Hensley survey, which bordered the Garza survey lands on the north. A son, Pitts Aikman, was born to them on December 13, 1868. Another son, William Smith Aikman, would join the family February 11, 1872.

An unusual event occurred when three of Louisa's daughters married the three sons of Washington S. Wallace: Sarah Ann Miller was married to Matthew Alexander Wallace in 1870. Then came marriages between Laura Jane Cohron and Robert Wiley Wallace, then Ellen Cohron and William W. Wallace.

At the time of the marriage between Sarah Ann Miller and Matthew Wallace, Sarah's sister, Celia Frances, deeded her inherited interest in the Miller estate to Sarah and Matthew. Thus they began married life on the 333-acre Robert T. Miller homestead on the Garza Survey on Tehuacana Creek.

Joseph Milam Lynch and Roxanna lived on the Lynch portion of the Garza survey that had been deeded him by his father. Also living on the Lynch land was his father-in-law, Washington S. Wallace, Margaret, A child, William Andrew Lynch, was born to Joseph Milam and Roxanna Lynch January 10, 1868. The child was named for Joseph's brother. Roxanna died in childbirth. A grieving Joseph M. Lynch then left the infant with Roxanna's parents and he went to Rapides Parish, near Alexandria, for comfort from his Neal relatives. While in Louisiana, he deeded to his infant son his one-half interest in the Garza survey lands.

William Andrew Lynch committed suicide April 3, 1868. He was despondent over his Civil War wounds that would not heal. His estate was in probate court for many years. His burial place is unknown. Meanwhile, the Wallace's continued to reside on the Miller-Lynch lands on Tehuacana Creek. Post-war Texas was in shambles. The Carpetbagger government assessed outrageous taxes on property and livestock. The herds of horses and cattle had grown in large numbers, but were practically worthless in the Texas marketplace.

These were troubled times, but they were going to be worse.

Lynch Headstones at Springfield Cemetery

The author is shown marking the graves of Mary Miller Lynch, who died in 1852, and her infant son Nathaniel Lynch, who died in 1847. The Lynch infant was the first recorded grave in Springfield Cemetery. The cemetery is now a part of Fort Park State Park near Groesbeck, Texas.

The 3x5 foot granite markers at right commemorates the service of Joseph Penn Lynch for his service to Texas during the revolutionary period. Lynch served during the battle of Bexar at San Antonio in 1835, and fought in the battle at San Jacinto where the Mexicans were defeated and Texas gained independence and became the Republic of Texas. The actual burial site of Lynch is unknown, but the Texas Historical Commission placed the marker on the family burial site in 1986 commemorating the Texas bicentennial of independence.

CARPETBAGGER GOVERNMENT
AND THE BIRTH OF THE COWBOY

The Civil War brought winds of change to Texas. Over the objections of Governor Sam Houston, the hero of San Jacinto, the legislature voted to secede from the Union and joined the Confederacy in the War Between the States. The Texas population had grown to 600,000 by 1860. More than 60,000 Texans had enlisted in the Confederate Army, while nearly 2,000 Texans were counted on the side of the Union.

Houston knew the South could not win a war with the industrialized North, and he was right. Initial victories by the confederates in the early stages of the war brought elation that was soon dashed when the superiority of the weaponry and rail networks of the North began to take a devastating toll on the southern forces.

Benjamin Posey, Bill Posey, Washington Wallace and Matthew Wallace answered the call to arms with the Confederacy. All were mustered in as privates in Company G, 4th Regiment of the Arizona Brigade. This regiment had been organized in Texas as the Baird's Cavalry Regiment, but had joined the Arizona Brigade. Their service was principally in the Texas areas and in the Indian Territory, where they were charged with keeping supply lines open between Fort Gibson to the north and Fort Towson to the south. This was a vital connection because some supplies moved over the Texas Road in the Territory and across the Red River into Texas.

The Indian tribes that had relocated to Indian Territory were divided in loyalty to the Civil War. Some became aligned with the South and some with the North. Some did not want any part of the war at all, believing it was a white man's war. Many moved to the Texas side of the Red River to escape the internal strife that enveloped their tribes and people.

The Texas unit serving in the Indian Territory had caused a reunion of the Posey's with their Creek relatives who had moved to the Territory during the Indian removal period of the 1830s. Bill

Posey became acquainted with the Indian lands and his relatives. Confederate Army records reveal that Bill Posey deserted December 9, 1865. Matt Wallace had deserted the year before. Benjamin Posey and Washington Wallace continued to serve as teamsters in the Confederate cause until the end of the war and the surrender of the Confederate forces. Bill Posey had become thoroughly familiar with the Indian Territory and his relatives. He would have occasion to return.

Texas had not seen any major battles on her soil during the war. Neither had the Indian Territory. Both had escaped the burning and pillage of the cities suffered by other states in the south. The Indians, however, suffered homestead burnings and livestock slaughters by their own kind. And their alignment with the confederacy would cost them dearly with Reconstruction following the northern victory in 1865.

Texas had never been wealthy as a Republic or as a state. The Civil War had drained the state budget and the budgets of the average household as well. Texans were land rich and cash poor. The cotton-based economy with slave labor was changed overnight with the freeing of the slaves. Cotton had been the principal cash crop, but now the fields lay idle and weeds had taken over the land. There wasn't enough labor to sustain the former cotton economy, and there was no cash with which to pay the former slaves for labor. The economic situation had left the landowner and the former slaves in a quandary.

Reconstruction following the war wreaked further havoc on the lives of Texans. The Carpetbagger government installed by the northern politicians had the state in chaos. Texas was under tight military control, and law and order was virtually non-existent. The federal government refused to allow any southern state to organize any body of armed men for any purpose, so the fabled Texas Rangers were reduced to a small, powerless band with little or no authority. There was still trouble with the Indians on the western front in Texas, but the job of keeping the Indians at bay fell to the forces of the regular Union Army, which did little to protect settlers in the established communities, or those expanding the Texas frontier to the west.

In 1869, Edmund J. Davis was elected as a Republican Carpetbagger Governor. Davis took office in January 1870, and immediately began a campaign to organize a state police force to deal with "a state filled with desperate characters." Davis pushed the bill through the legislature, and in July 1870 the State Police Force was organized.

The "force" was comprised to a large degree, by Negro officers who had only months before, been slaves. At the head were appointees favorable to the Union cause. The citizenry complained that the State Police were being unfair in their dispensation of justice. Many complained that the "haughty" Negro police who, they said, were merely trying to extract "justice" for the past social policies was unduly arresting former slave owners

At the end of the first month of the Davis term, he announced the arrest of 44 murderers and felons by the State Police. Five had been killed while resisting arrest, Davis said. A scandal erupted when Adjutant General James Davidson, head of the State Police, suddenly resigned and left the post, and the state, with $34,000 in public funds. An undaunted Governor Davis persisted with his so-called Law-and-order policies, which included inflicting heavy tax penalties on property owners if the citizens dared defy the State Police. Citizens of many counties rose up in protest. Lynching of many of the Negro State Police officers was common. In each case Davis was quick to pronounce martial law and inflict his heavy tax burden on the people.

In an October 1871 bar room incident, a Negro policeman in Limestone County shot and severely wounded a Groesbeck citizen, D.C. Applewhite. Applewhite staggered across the street and fell, mortally wounded. One of the Negro police followed him across the street and pumped two more bullets into his body, killing him. An outraged citizenry quickly organized a force of armed men, causing the Negroes to seek sanctuary in the mayor's office.

There they barricaded themselves, fired shots into the streets and defied arrest by the enraged mob. About 20 associates who had secured horses soon rescued the deputies, and the group rode out of town. The steaming Davis promptly declared martial law in Limestone County and adjoining Freestone County, and assessed a penalty of $50,000 on property owners in the two counties. The penalty was to be paid by an additional three percent tax. Armed deputies were dispatched to each farm to collect the tax.

Governor Davis and his Carpetbagger courts also came under severe criticism by the citizens. In many cases prisoners were kept in jail for long periods of time while the Carpetbagger courts filed repeated continuances. One prisoner, it was said, was brought a lunch by his wife which contained a peach. After eating the peach, he dropped the seed out the window and on the ground. The peach seed took sprout. It was said the prisoner was in jail so long that he was eating peaches picked from a tree that grew by the bars of his cell from the seed dropped years before.

This unsettled scenario had a profound effect on the lives of all Texans. A severe depression gripped the state on farm commodities, and high taxes inflicted by the Carpetbagger government were devastating. A bright spot was recognized in the Texas cattle market, however, but not at home. Texas cattle were practically worthless on the local market, but huge profits awaited those who were able to get beef to the northern markets. There was only one obstacle--how to get them there. What few miles of Texas rail line that had been laid before the war had come to a halt during the conflict, and no rails at all existed running north and south. The nearest connection point of rails to the northern market lay several hundred miles to the north at Abilene, Kansas.

Texas cattle had been successfully driven overland via the Shawnee Trail in the 1840s. The trail led from near present Dallas northeasterly across the Red River, through the Indian Territory, to a connecting railhead at Kansas City, Missouri. But the Civil War and a Missouri quarantine against the tick-fever-bearing Longhorns had closed the Shawnee Trail route years before. The insatiable

Yankee appetite for beef following the war caused a renewed interest in providing Texas beef to satisfy the potential market.

Attention now turned to the Chisholm Trail, which had been established by Jesse Chisholm in 1867. Chisholm was a Scot-Cherokee resident of the Indian Territory. Trusted by both the whites and the Indians, he traveled freely among all the tribes and was welcomed wherever he went. He had established a trading post along the Canadian River in the center of Indian Territory. Chisholm had successfully moved cattle over the trail from Texas to the Kansas railhead, where he received top dollar for the animals. There were no quarantines against Texas cattle at Abilene, and word was out that they welcomed the cowboy and the cattle.

The Posey's and Wallace's were quick to seize upon the new opportunities that lay to the north. Their herds of cattle and horses had increased tremendously on the open range of Texas. They were all experienced in raising and tending cattle. They had supplied horses from their large herd to the army during the war, but this market had dried up. Cattle were worth a scant three dollars per head on the local market, but worth bring $20 to $30 per head at Abilene.

From economic necessity was born the American cowboy. The cowboy was not born an infant, however. He was dumped on the Texas plains full-grown, clawing and scratching for survival. He was lean and mean, and tough as rawhide from suffering through wars, famine and economic disaster. The Posey and Wallace boys fit in well.

The change from the cotton economy to cattle raising would result in a new dress, vocabulary and new way of life for the Tehuacana settlers. The loose-fitting garments of the farmer were replaced with tight shirts and trousers. The Texans now adopted a manner and dress the Mexican vaqueros had practiced for generations. Leather chaps protected their legs against the cutting thorns of brush and mesquite. Large wide-brimmed hats protected against the burning Texas sun, and rawhide plaited ropes adorned their saddles. The Spanish names of the *vaquero* also stuck; *lariat, chaps, remuda, pancho,* and *sombrero.* Their boots now had a pointed toe and high heel to fit easily into the saddle stirrup. The tops went to the knees for added protection when riding in the brush.

The change would hold great promise for the families, but dark clouds were gathering on the horizon.

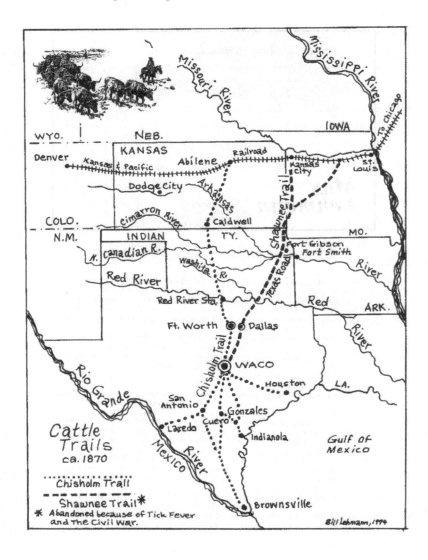

Max Lehmann: German Cowboy

Seeking change and adventure from his disciplined German work ethic; Max Lehmann found it as a cowboy. Born in Germany in 1854, he came to Indianola, Texas, in 1854 with his father, Carl Ludwig Gustav Lehmann, and his brother, Paul, age two. The wife and mother, Adelphine Louisa Sperling died in Germany or on board ship to America. Gustav, Paul and Max settled at Indianola, where Gustav was an employee of the Morgan Steamship Lines.

Lehmann joined the M.M. Halliburton ranch out of Gonzales at age 16 and helped drive cattle to the marketplace at New Orleans, Louisiana. The opening of the Chisholm Trail through Indian Territory to the Kansas railroads offered great opportunity to ease the economic depression and devastation most Texas families experienced following the Civil War. Max Lehmann and the Halliburton crew rounded up Longhorn cattle from the mesquite thickets around Gonzales and Cuero. It was not an easy job as the cattle were determined not to wind up as steaks on some Yankee dinner table. After gathering the cattle, Max and the other Texas cowboys had to swallow pounds of chocking dust; ford swollen rivers; be chilled by sudden rainstorms; be pounded by hail and survive ferocious lightning storms in driving the cattle more than 1,000 miles to Kansas.

It was on the cattle drives through Waco Max met and married Sarah Ann (Miller) Wallace, who had been widowed when her husband was lynched in 1873. Max and Sarah raised her two Wallace children and had six of their own, one of which was Will Lehmann, father of the author. Sarah died in 1900. Max was murdered in 1904 near Carrizo Springs, Texas. The killer spent a year in jail but was released because of lack of evidence, he being the only surviving witness. Lehmann's body or burial place has yet to be discovered.

(Photo circa 1890 from the Jesse Halliburton collection

TROUBLE WITH THE LAW

Texas cattle were easy pickings. Vast herds of longhorns grazed peacefully in the mesquite brush all over central and south Texas. They were the mavericks that had escaped the Spanish explorers and the Mexicans. They roamed freely over the plains and multiplying rapidly. Every mesquite bush seemed to have a longhorn behind it.

Barbed wire would not be invented until 1874 and would not be in widespread use until the late 1880s. The "estray law" prevailed on the open range. Cattle roaming without a brand could be claimed by anyone catching the animal and advertising possession. If no one claimed it, the animal belonged to the catcher. Few paid any serious attention to the estray law, and vast herds were gathered from the brush to be pushed north to the markets. Few herds existed that did not first bear the brands of others.

The area around Waco was suddenly becoming a major collection point for the cattle being rounded up in south central Texas and driven north. The Wallace and Posey spreads on the Tehuacana had become the center of activity. Cattle from the ranges of San Antonio, Houston, Victoria, Cuero, Gonzales, Corpus Christi and Brownsville were herded north and funneled into Waco. From there they were driven north over a single trail to Fort Worth and the Chisholm Trail. The trail then traversed to the western lands of Indian Territory where it reached the subsequent Kansas market.

The Wallace and Posey lands were at the small end of the funnel where the cattle crossed the Brazos River and headed north. Waco was a major crossing on the Brazos. A ferry existed there but was used very little for the crossing of cattle. The river was deep and wide, and the cattle were swum across--a dangerous maneuver for the stock, horse and rider.

Waco had 3,000 inhabitants in the 1870 census. Though small, the town was showing its importance, and growth was imminent.

The town had furnished six generals and five colonels to the Confederate Army, and this leadership extended to civic affairs. The newly created cattle market was having an impact on the local economy, and business leaders were making plans for future growth.

A charter was granted by the state in 1866 to build a permanent toll bridge over the Brazos River at Waco. Even with money scarce and interest rates high during Reconstruction, the Waco Bridge Company sold all its stock. In mid 1868 the company chose J.A. Roebling & Son of Trenton, New Jersey to design and build a new suspension-type bridge. Roebling was the designer and builder of New York's Brooklyn Bridge that would be built later. The Waco Bridge was on a much smaller scale, but the design and style were the same.

WACO SUSPENSION BRIDGE,

Built in 1868, the bridge is still in use today.

Work on the bridge began in September 1868. Waco had no machine shops or any artisans with the necessary skills to build a bridge of such magnitude. The nearest railroad was 100 miles away. The woven wire cables and other bridge components were shipped by steamer to Galveston, where they were transferred to rail bound for Bryan, then taken by ox wagons on a rutted, dusty road to Waco. The bridge was completed in late December 1869. The first toll was collected January 1, 1870. The bridge had cost

$141,000 and was the first bridge to cross the Brazos River. The main span was wide enough for two stagecoaches to pass each other, and it was 475 feet long, with heavy oak planks for flooring. Not only did the company charge people to cross, but also collected five cents for every head of cattle that passed over the span. Activity from the southern end of the Chisholm Trail funneled in large herds of cattle, which crossed the bridge and helped the company retire its debt. Most drovers could not afford such a heavy toll and chose the cheaper alternative of swimming their herds across the Brazos.

Bill Posey and Matt Wallace were extremely adept at this newly created cowboy life. They were both small in stature, about five-foot-seven, lean and quick as lightning. Posey's appearance did reveal his Indian heritage. He was brown skinned, with dark flashing eyes. His hair was dark and coarse. He burned well in the Texas sun, however, and carried a deep tan. Wallace was of about the same complexion, only with darker eyes. At times he was clean-shaven, but sometimes he wore a heavy, dark mustache.

To catch a Longhorn steer for branding or doctoring was difficult. They could not use the technique that would bring the animal to the ground with a rope and tripping because the long horns would be subject to breakage very easily. The preferred method was for Posey to catch the head and Wallace the hind feet. The horses would then go in opposite directions, stretching out the animal more gently, where a branding iron could be applied before the release.

The Wallace and Posey families were becoming more active in gathering cattle. They went into the south Texas mesquite thickets and increased their herds, which they drove to the homestead near Waco. There they sorted and branded the strays, allowing them to graze for a while as the herd size increased and they could be driven to market. Posey's father, Benjamin F. Posey, had a ranch at Horn Hill, east of the Brazos River in Limestone County. Their collective herds stretched from the Brazos back into Freestone County to the east.

In the spring, a round up began, and the herds were driven north into Fort Worth. The cattle then went to Doan's Crossing on the Red River, north across the river and into Indian Territory, and finally into Abilene, Kansas where they were sold. The trip took 90 days with good luck, longer if they encountered swollen rivers or other troubles along the trail.

The Wallace and Posey families had managed to survive through some difficult times during the war and Reconstruction. The northern market for beef was showing promise for better times. Finally they were accumulating some cash money and buying more land. But troubles loomed ahead as they began getting into trouble with the law.

Matt Wallace had been appointed as a road overseer on a portion of the road that was being built from Waco to Corsicana. The road ran along the south boundary line of the Wallace and Posey lands, but Wallace was responsible for several miles of the road. His duties were to maintain the roads and the bridges that crossed Tehuacana Creek.

Some of Wallace's neighbors were complaining that he was neglecting his road duties for the livestock operation. The charge was so serious that a grand jury was empanelled for the spring term of court in 1869 to look into the allegations. After hearing evidence, the grand jury indicted Wallace in cause No. 1005, for "failure of duty as a road overseer." The charge was filed in the 33rd Judicial Court of the 19th District, McLennan County. His neighbors, Dr. S.A. Owens, William Warwick and Col. S.J. Strother, signed the complaint. Wallace was arrested on the charge and bond posted. Wallace's attorney successfully defended him on the charges, saying the charge was merely a misdemeanor and not a felony. Charges were dismissed.

Also in the 1869 spring term of court, the grand jury indicted Matt's younger brother, William W. Wallace on a charge of assault with intent to murder. William Wallace was only 19 at the time. The indictment charged that on the eighth of June, 1869, Wallace did "with force and arms in McLennan County, upon the body of

George Green, feloniously, willfully and with malice, assault with a six-shooting pistol in his right hand, did beat, strike and wound with intent to kill and murder the said George Green." State's witnesses in the Cause No. 945 were B.L. Taylor and George Green. Wallace failed to appear at the summer term of court, and Matt Wallace and W.G. Coats forfeited bonds in the amount of $200 dollars. The charges were dismissed in 1874 because the state's witnesses had never been located.

The youngest Wallace brother, Robert, 18, was indicted June 10, 1871, with a charge of intent to kill, on the body of one James Vaught. The Charge, Cause No. 1406, stated that on February 25, 1871 "Robert Wallace, with a six-shooting pistol, cocked, did strike James Vaught with intent to kill and murder. The said Robert Wallace was aided and abetted by William W. Wallace in the felony aforesaid." Attempts were made several times to serve subpoenas. The defendants could not be found on two occasions, and the plaintiff could not be found on two other occasions. The court vacated the charge April 8, 1872.

The roof fell in as the horse and cattle operations came under scrutiny. Posey was indicted October 1, 1870, for violation of the estray law, having in his possession a black gelding with a brand belonging to Thomas Edwards of Freestone County. Indictments were also issued in other causes against W.S. Wallace, Matt Wallace, William W. Wallace, Robert W. Wallace and Posey--all for violation of the estray law. Specific charges were named in altering cattle brands, theft of horses, cattle and oxen belonging to others.

Posey was individually cited for most of the offenses. He hired the law firm of Coke, Herring and Anderson as attorneys for his defense, and pleaded not guilty. The Wallace's, named only on a few indictments, posted bond, and the cases were continued.

Richard Coke, Posey's lawyer, successfully defended him on four counts of horse and cattle theft with juries returning verdicts of not guilty. But his luck ran out. Cause No. 1381, filed in the district court at Waco in the August term, 1871, charged Posey with the theft of two beef steers, valued at ten dollars per head. The cattle belonged to M.J. Sanderson of McLennan County. Posey, his father, Benjamin Posey, and his brother-in-law, James W. Allen posted Bond in the amount of $200 dollars. Posey was released on bond to await trial before Judge J.W. Oliver.

The case came before the jury and Judge Oliver on May 2, 1872. Posey's attorneys, Coke, Herring and Anderson filed a plea to the judge saying, "the defendant asks the court to charge the jury that the fact of cattle belonging to others being found in a drove belonging to the defendant even in defendant's mark and brand does not raise a presumption of guilt, if the evidence shows that the herd was in charge of others, unless it is shown that the defendant knew the cattle were in the herd or authorized them to be put in." Judge Oliver refused the plea, and the case went before the jury.

After hearing the evidence, the jury was retired for a verdict with these hand-written instructions to the jurors: "Gentlemen of the jury: If you believe from the evidence that the defendant fraudulently took the two steers, property of Mr. Sanderson, as charged in the indictment with the intent to deprive Mr. Sanderson of their value and to appropriate the same to the defendants own use and benefit, you will find the defendant guilty. If the property so taken is of the value of 20 or more dollars you will assess his punishment as imprisonment in the penitentiary any length of time not less than two years, nor more than five years. But if you find the property was of less value than $20 you will assess his punishment as imprisonment in the county jail any length of time not to exceed two years and you may in addition to such imprisonment assess a fine against the defendant not to exceed $100, or you can imprison without fining, but you can fine without imprisonment.

"And gentlemen, if you do not believe that the defendant is guilty you will say so by your verdict. I charge you further that if you believe the defendant had in his possession the oxen at any time and was driving them to market without a written bill of sale from the owner, the law says he is guilty. You will also find unless the defendant shows you evidence that he came honestly by the property. If you are not satisfied beyond a doubt that the property was worth 20 or more dollars you cannot penitentiary him, but if he is guilty of the theft of the property you can assess his punishment by imprisonment in jail and fine, or by imprisonment without the fine as heretofore instructed. J.W. Oliver, Judge."

After hearing the evidence the jury returned a verdict of guilty. They apparently found the value at less than $20 dollars, for the jury assessed Posey's punishment at three months in the county jail and a fine of $100. The verdict was signed by M.E. McLaren, foreman. Posey was released on bond to await formal sentencing by the court.

The December 1871, court term was Posey's undoing, however. He had been charged in July with the theft of two mules, and the Cause No. 1436 was coming to trial. The official indictment read that "one W.A. Posey in July 1871, with force and arms in McLennan County, steal one brown mule (unbranded), of the value of $100, and one light-bay horse mule, (unbranded), of the value of $100, of the goods, chattels and property of David McFadden, then and there being found, then and there, fraudulently and feloniously, did steal, take and carry away from the possession of said owner, without the consent of the owner thereof, with intent to deprive the said owner of the value of the same, and to appropriate the said property to the use and benefit of him, the said W.A. Posey, contrary to the form of the statute in such case made and provided, and against the peace and dignity of the State. Signed: P.M. McClelland, Foreman of the Grand Jury." Witnesses for the prosecution were listed as Gilbert Scott, David McFadden, Robert Jasper, W.W. Kirkland and Hiram Roose.

Trial was scheduled for December 15, but witnesses crucial to the prosecution did not show for the trial. The judge issued orders to the sheriff to serve subpoenas to John Cantaloe, J. Cantaloe, Richard Stanfield, D. Harris, Scott Farrell and John France to appear in the next term of court in January, 1872. The sheriff returned the service papers stating that he found J. Cantaloe and

Richard Stanfield, but the others could not be found.

The judge also issued orders to the sheriff ordering attachment of witness Hiram Roose, "who is today at Bill Posey's place killing hogs." The order instructed the officers to "take good bond for his appearance at the next term of court." Word must have traveled fast to Hiram Roose, who had stopped killing hogs and vanished by the time the sheriff arrived at Posey's house, just a few miles east of Waco.

Enough witnesses had been rounded up for the April 1872, term of court. The trial went as scheduled, before a judge and jury. After hearing the evidence, the jury retired for its verdict. The jury soon returned and the foreman, B. F. Richey, presented the findings to the judge: "We the jury, find the defendant guilty as charged in the indictment, and assess his punishment at hard labor in the state penitentiary for the term of five years."

The verdict and sentence was devastating to Posey, who at age 26 would have to leave his wife and three small boys while he served the sentence. The charges were far more serious than violating an estray law. Cattle roaming freely on the range were subject to being added to a herd with little question. Mules and oxen were a different thing, however. These were the work animals on a farm and were not allowed to roam. They were kept behind the split-rail fences and fed corn. Woe be to the man who had these animals in his possession without a bill of sale. Posey was released on bond and ordered to appear May 12, 1872, for formal sentencing.

The day for formal sentencing arrived, but Posey did not. He had taken to the wilderness some said, near his father's ranch. Posey had holed up in the "Posey Thicket" near the ranch in the Tehuacana hills. There was not a man in all Limestone County brave enough to go in and get Posey.

The court, after several delays, finally declared Posey a fugitive from justice, and an arrest warrant was issued June 14, 1872. There were 16 more indictments against Posey yet to be heard. Apprehension and arrest of Posey would not be an easy task.

He knew the country like the back of his hand. He had roamed far and wide in gathering up cattle and had many friends, some of whom were also on the edge of the law. But Posey not only had trouble with the law, there was trouble in the family as well.

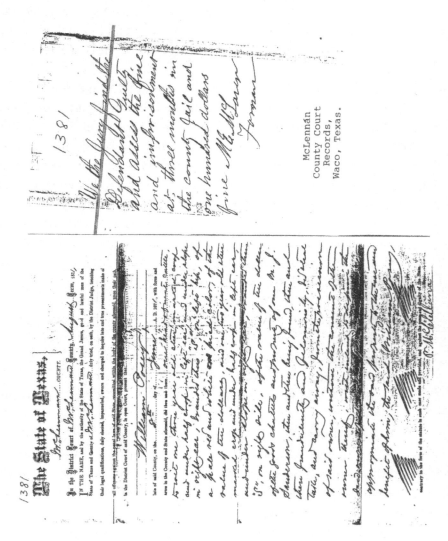

McLennán
County Court
Records,
Waco, Texas.

McLennan County
Court Records,
Waco, Texas.

TERROR ON THE TEHUACANA

Sarah Ann Wallace had inherited a portion of the Garza Survey from her deceased father, Robert T. Miller, who had bought the land in 1846. With a deed from her sister, Celia, also an heir, Sarah and Matt Wallace began married life with 333 acres of this choice Tehuacana Creek bottomland. They were married in 1869. One child, Sarah Emmaline, had been born in 1871.

On February 24, 1871, Posey bought the Wallace property for a sum of $4,500. He signed a note to pay the Wallace's $1,000 dollars a year for five years in payment for the land. Matthew and Sarah then purchased the 160 acre Cohron survey land in Limestone County from her mother, Louisa, and Sarah's half-sisters, Ellen and Laura Jane. Posey's ambition for land ownership also caused him to buy on June 24, 1871, a 600 acre tract on the Thomas de la Vega survey for $5,000. This land was located west of the Garza survey, near Waco, at the Brazos River.

With Posey's conviction on the theft charges and being a fugitive from justice, the note payments to the Wallace's were now in jeopardy. The fate of the land was then sealed with the filings of civil action lawsuits against Posey.

Cause No. 2081 was filed in the December 1872, term of court by Dr. S.A. Owens against Posey, seeking $272.50 for medicines and services rendered by the plaintiff, as physician, during the year of 1870. The suit also sought payment for medicines and services rendered in 1871 for $273 ollars. In addition, the petition alleged that bond monies in the amount of $140 dollars had been advanced Posey by the doctor for Posey's legal troubles on the theft charges. He had also lent Posey $100 dollars in gold coin on July 12, 1871, which had not been repaid on the due date. The suit asked for judgment in the amounts presented by the doctor.

Dr. Sherwood A. Owens was a neighbor to the Wallace's and Posey's. This is the same person who had signed the complaint against Matt Wallace in the alleged neglect of duty as road overseer. Owens was born in Logan County, Kentucky in July

1819. He graduated from Kemper College at St. Louis, Mo., in 1840. Having determined his future in medicine, he began reading under the direction of a physician in St. Louis, receiving a medical diploma from Missouri University. In 1844 he went to Philadelphia, where he entered the University of Pennsylvania, obtaining his medical degree in 1846.

Answering the call for soldiers in the Mexican war of 1847, he entered Texas serving as an assistant surgeon with the U.S. Army. Following the defeat of the Mexicans by U.S. forces, Owens then located in New Orleans where he practiced medicine for a time. In 1849 he went to Missouri where he joined a party of friends who were about to cross the plains to California. The 128-day trip was made without incident. He opened an office in San Francisco, but in less than a year journeyed to Australia where he practiced medicine and invested in mining. He served as a surgeon for one year with the British army in the Crimean war.

Owens returned to the United States locating again in Missouri. He married in 1856 and came to Waco, then a village of 5000 people, in 1858. At the outbreak of the Civil War in 1861, Owens enlisted as a surgeon in the Confederate Army. Following the war he returned to Waco and was engaged in medicine and real estate.

The Owens case against Posey came before the jury on July 2, 1873. The jury awarded $957 dollars to Owens, plus eight percent interest per annum, and court costs of the lawsuit. The court attached 272 head of stock cattle owned by Posey, which were seized by Constable W.H. Jones, of Hill County. The cattle were sold, but the court noted the sale price was not sufficient to satisfy the judgment of the suit.

The court ordered seizure of another 290 head of stock cattle owned by Posey. In addition, the court had ordered seizure of 133 and 1/3 acres of land on July 10, 1872, subject to the judgment. The land was to be divided into tracts of not more than 40 acres and sold to satisfy the judgment of the court.

Posey's financial problems increased when another filing in

the December 1872 court term by Coke, Herring and Anderson, sought the amount of $448.46 to satisfy a note signed by Posey and his wife, Elizabeth. The note had been signed May 1, 1872, for legal fees in the defense of Posey, and was to be repaid before the following September, according to the petition. Posey had since become a fugitive and was not present when the court awarded the amount asked, plus interest at eight percent per annum plus all costs of the court action. The court also seized 333 acres of the Posey land, ordering the sheriff to advertise and sell the land in 40-acre tracts until the amount divided "shall amount to sufficient to pay off and discharge said amount of judgment, interest and costs."

Posey's conviction and sentence and the loss of the Tehuacana Creek lands ended what dreams the Matthew Wallace and Bill Posey families had of building a successful ranching operation. Posey was at large, and the Wallace's lost land they had never been paid for—Sarah Ann Miller's inheritance.

Bill Posey's presence was still being felt in McLennan and Limestone counties even though he was at large. Many said he was at the head of a gang that was active in rustling and terrorizing the area. The State Police force activated by Governor Davis was a failure. Crime was on the increase in the Waco area, and several murders had been committed. Newspaper articles of the day told of ranch families afraid to venture out after dark. The rustlers were even getting so bold as to steal horses and cattle in broad daylight, according to published reports.

Receiving a tip that Posey was in the area to visit his wife and children, Sheriff Morris and a posse lay in wait for the fugitive on the Corsicana road, near his home. As Posey crossed Tehuacana Creek, the lawmen stepped out of their concealment in the brush and ordered him to give up. Realizing the men had the drop on him and being alone, Posey reluctantly surrendered to the authorities and was placed in jail at Waco.

Concern for law and order reached a feverish pitch in the county when a gang boldly broke into the county jail at Waco on the night of June 1, 1873, releasing Posey and three other prisoners--two convicted murderers. The freed prisoners were Posey, convicted on the mule theft charge; John Smith, convicted on a second degree murder charge and sentenced to seventeen years in the state penitentiary; William Fulcher, convicted of second degree murder and sentenced to 10 years; and George Stockman, sentenced to five years in the state pen for the theft of a gelding. All were awaiting transfer to the state pen at Huntsville.

Law officers and newspaper reports claimed Bill Posey had a hand in the jailbreak. Court records do not reveal any charges lodged against Posey in the affair, but Posey was again on the loose, and McLennan County residents would not rest easily at night.

A scene of terror unfolded on a dark night June 12, 1873, when a group of men approached the home of Matt and Sarah Ann Wallace who had moved to Waco. Breaking into the house, the masked mob woke the sleeping family and overpowered Wallace. Dragging him outside, they proceeded to an oak tree in the front yard, where his hands were tied behind him. They placed the struggling Wallace upon the back of a horse and threw a rope around his neck. With a hard slap on the rump of the horse, the animal bolted, leaving a writhing Matt Wallace dangling, with a broken neck. The tree was not tall enough to allow a full fall, so a member of the mob placed a rope around his feet and stretched him out, making sure he was dead.

This morbid scene occurred before the terrified eyes of Sarah and their two-year old daughter. The shouting mob left a sobbing Sarah Ann Wallace collapsed on the ground beneath her slain husband, as their bewildered daughter, Sarah Emmaline grasped for comfort from her mother. The grieving Sarah was also six months pregnant with the couple's second child at the time of the lynching.

The *Dallas Herald* of July 12, 1873, told of the incident under a one-line heading slugged "Lynch Law:"

"The *Waco Examiner* of the first, brings us the accounts of the hanging, by a disguised mob, of Mat. Wallace, who was a brother-in-law of the celebrated Bill Posey, who has figured extensively as a horse man in that portion of the state. His transactions in horseflesh were not always on the square, and the people tiring of his style of horse-trading have taken this summary manner to rid themselves of him. We are no friend to midnight murderers, and condemn most heartily anything that has not the sanction as well as the coloring of the law, in treating the rights that ought to belong to everyone. Mat. Wallace may have been a terror to his section, but we dare say he had a greater right to fear his neighbors than they him, as the facts prove. Good men may sometimes become disgusted with the law's delays, but they should never allow themselves to become desperate to the extent of shedding the blood of a fellow creature without according to him every right our constitution grants to the citizens of Texas."

Newspaper accounts describe the Wallace lynching as being committed by his neighbors, and later newspaper accounts claimed Wallace was strung up with the assistance of his own brother-in-law, Bill Posey. Court records for McLennan County from 1870 through 1880 do not show anyone was ever officially charged with the murder of Matt Wallace. A newspaper article published in the *Waco Examiner* February 22, 1877, told of the arrest of a William Crabtree for "complicity in the murder of Matthew Wallace, who was hung by Bill Posey's gang in the suburbs of the city in 1873."

Examination of court records show that Crabtree was actually arrested and charged with a knife attack on another person, a charge of which he was later acquitted. Crabtree was a Limestone County punk who had faced many charges of rustling and horse theft all over Central Texas. There is reason to believe both Posey and Crabtree took part in the hanging of Matt Wallace, but they were never officially charged in court--only in the newspapers. Lawmen and Wallace family members were quick to point accusing fingers at both Posey and Crabtree, but proving the accusations was another matter.

Concerning the jailbreak, officers did recognize four men who were officially charged with "rescuing and releasing prisoners from jail." Cause No. 1991, which was filed July 29, 1873, charged Pink Smith, John Swift, Charles Wilcox and Bill Smith with the offense. Witnesses to the jailbreak were Mrs. William Vaughn, Mrs. Swift, L.D. Reed and Harvey Wilson. Warrants were issued to sheriffs in several counties. On July 30, Pink Smith was arrested in Falls County and placed in jail. The others had scattered.

Another event calling attention to the growing lawlessness around Waco occurred shortly after the jailbreak and the lynching of Wallace. Deputy Sheriff Burt Blankenship was gunned down in a confrontation with a band of armed men just on the outskirts of the city. A story in the *Waco Examiner* of July 25, 1873, told the story:

"THE WACO MURDER. Another foul murder was committed last night within a few miles of this city, by the Tehuacana outlaws in McLennan County. In the early part of yesterday these ruffians appeared within some three miles of the city, and the Deputy Sheriff with a posse started immediately to arrest them, dividing his forces into squads of three to five men.

"Immediately after dark one of them encountered some men lying in ambush. Burt Blankenship, a good citizen, who for some time has been acting as Deputy Sheriff, and who has hitherto taken a very active part in the effort to bring these outlaws to justice, was at the head of the squad. He halted and demanded, "Who are you?" The men in the ambush made no reply. Blankenship then said: "If you don't answer me, I'll fire!" The response was a volley, one shot hitting Deputy Blankenship in the breast and mortally wounding him. He died within a half hour after being hit. Prior to his death, he recognized his murderer, one Bob Chrystal, who has been a terror to the people of Waco and the surrounding neighborhood.

"This Chrystal is the same man who headed the gang that released the prisoners from jail a few weeks ago, and is suspected of being involved in the recent lynching of Matt Wallace. He is a noted stock thief, and he and his gang have threatened to take the lives of several of the best citizens in the county. Fear of him and his gang have forced these citizens to keep men on duty every night for a month past, to protect them from the nocturnal incursions of this gang of desperadoes. The murder of Deputy Sheriff Blankenship has created considerable excitement here, and decisive steps will be taken to arrest and bring them to justice.

"For this reason, the court, which was in session, adjourned, so that the grand jury and other officials could lend their aid in the capture. Over 100 men have already left on the trail, and a great many men from surrounding counties will join them.

"Last night, two horses, saddles, and a pistol and one six-shooter were found. They are supposed to belong to the murderous gang.

"It is rumored that one of the assassins was captured today. Public indignation runs so high that if any of them are captured, it is barely possible they will trouble the courts."

The brazen murders of Wallace and Blankenship, and the open defiance of the law by the renegades in McLennan County caused great public alarm and indignation. The July term of court was abruptly terminated, and a special session of the court and the naming of a special grand jury were immediately called to deal with the growing criminal problem. The July Special Term of 1873 was called for the 19th District Court, 33rd Judicial District at the courthouse in Waco. The jury, after reviewing the evidence presented was seated Tuesday morning, July 29, and presented these indictments to the court:

"On this day comes into open court the Honorable Grand Jury and through the foreman, there being present fourteen of their number, and makes the following presentation of indictments, to-wit:

"Cause No. 1990. The State of Texas vs. John Swift, Charge: Murder.

"Cause No. 1991, the State of Texas vs. Pinch Smith, John Swift, Charles Wilcox and Bill Smith. Charge: Rescuing prisoners from the county jail."

The jury also presented the following memorial to Judge Blanton of the 33rd Judicial District:

"Sir: Lawlessness has pervaded to an alarming extent in our county, but we find the crimes have mostly been committed by transient parties, and we would respectfully ask Your Honor petition the Governor to offer such reward as necessary to insure the capture of the outlaws John Swift, W.A. Posey and John Smith. Upon investigation, we find that the outlaw Bob Crystal met his death at the hands of the Sheriff's posse in the lawful discharge of their duty. T.H. Killingsworth, Foreman of the Grand Jury."

The grand jury report indicated the killing of the outlaw Bob Crystal, whom the slain deputy Blankenship had identified as his assailant before he died. The newspaper article on the death of Blankenship made no mention of the death of Crystal, but it must have happened shortly after the deputies were in pursuit of the outlaws who had killed Blankenship.

The Grand Jury named John Swift as the murderer of Deputy Blankenship in indictment No. 1990, which was filed of record July 29, 1873: "And so the Grand Jurors aforesaid do say that the said John Swift--him the said Burwell Blankenship--in the manner and by the means aforesaid unlawfully--willfully--feloniously and of his malice aforethought did kill and murder--contrary to the form of the Statute in such case made and provided, and against the peace and dignity of the State. Signed, T.H. Killingsworth, Foreman of the Grand Jury."

Posey and the other escaped prisoners were causing great concern to some citizens of Waco, particularly M.D. Herring of the Coke, Herring and Anderson law firm. Also terrified for their personal safety were Dr. S.A. Owens and Charles Pearson, the McLennan County District attorney. Posey, with several of his friends, paid late night visits to the homes of Herring and Owens. Both said Posey threatened to kill them because of the civil lawsuits that caused the loss of his lands and livestock.

Governor Davis received urgent communications from the district attorney and Herring. The district attorney's letter urged the Governor to increase the reward posted on Posey to $1,000 in an effort to speed his capture. Herring's letter, dated July 3, 1873, enclosed copies of Posey's conviction and sentence, and requested the governor to authorize him (Herring) to "take his body and lodge the same in the said jail of said county." Posey "is now, or in a short time will be, in the Indian Territory, having recently left here for that section," the letter said. The letter pleaded for an immediate reply.

In a letter dated July 4, 1873, Pearson, the district attorney for the 33rd judicial district, appealed to the governor to take speedy action to secure the capture of Posey. Included in the Pearson letter was a communication dated June 26, 1873, from Captain Tiger, of the Creek Lighthorse in the Indian Territory, inquiring about the $1,000 reward being offered for Posey in Texas. The letter requested a description of the fugitive if the reward offer were genuine, Captain Tiger wrote.

Pearson's letter concluded with the observation that "This man Posey is a perfect terror to this community. It is supposed that he hung M.A. Wallace in Waco a short time ago. A few nights ago was at M.D. Herring's house at night with his party with a view to kill him, whose life he has threatened. He has also threatened to kill Dr. S.A. Owens of Waco. Please let me hear from you as early as you conveniently can," the letter pleaded.

The killing of Bob Crystal by the sheriff's deputies and the capture of Pinch Smith and Bill Smith had a calming effect on Waco and its citizens for a time. It was an uneasy calm, however. Bill Posey was still on the loose and raising hell in other parts of Texas. He was mean, and many citizens of Limestone and McLennan Counties had felt the terror of his threats. They would not rest easy until he was either jailed or killed. And the sooner the better!

Waco Tex, July 3 d/73

Gov. E.J. Davis.
  Austin Texa,
            Dear Sir –
            Herewith I enclose to you
certified copies of indictment and
judgment thereon now on file in the
District Court of McLennan County
against Bill Posey. who, I understand, is now probably, or in a short
time will be, in the Indian Territory,
having recently left here for that
section – My object in writing is
to ask a requisition of you on
authorizing me to take his body
and lodge the same in the jail
of said County –
            This matter demands prompt
attention – Please let me hear
from you immediately,
            Very Respectfully Yr. M. D. Herring

Sir

I understand there is a reward offered of $1000.00 One thousand
dollars for a man by the name of Bill
Posey - or W. A. Posey. If there is such
a reward offered please let me know-
and give me a description of him

Respectfully yours

N. B.   (Signed) Moty Tiger
Direct to Okmurge - Capt Light Horse Dep_y Clerk
    Creek Nation,   Creek Nation Ind Ty."
The following endorsements were on the
envelope. "County Sheriff -
            Waco
                Texas "

I wrote to your Excellency some time
ago - requesting you to increase the
reward for Posey's apprehension. to
$1000.00 I think if the reward is in
creased to $1000.00 he can and will be
brought in - If you increase the reward - please send me a copy - also a

110

copy of the former reward, properly
certified to. This man Posey is
a perfect terror to this community
it is supposed that he hung-
M A Wallace in Waco a short
time ago - and a few nights
ago - he it is supposed - was -
at Capt. M D Herrings house at
night with his party - with a
view to Kill him - Whose life
he has threatened - He has also
threatened to Kill Dr S. A Owens
of Waco - Please let me hear
from you - as early as you
conveniently. Can -
             Your obt Servt,
             Chas, B. Pearre
       deit. al. 35 — ? Au d deit

Documents from the Governor E. J. Davis collection, Texas State Library and Archives, Austin, Texas.

Waco July 4th 1873,

Edmd J Davis
    Gov of Texas
        Austin City

                        Sir

            The Sheriff of

McLennan County: received

a letter bearing date June

26th 1873 of which the following

is a true copy

            Okmulgee C.N. I.T. June 26th 73.

County
    Sheriff Waco Texas

WACO ADVANCE EXTRA.

TUESDAY, APRIL 7, 1872.

STOP THE MADMAN!

We believe the true solution of the course of the atrocities of Oliver are to be found in the suggestions of his diseased mind. We believe the man to be little better than a raving maniac, and that his proper place would be the insane asylum—and this opinion is substantiated by reliable medical authority. His frightful abuse of power, his ever-recurring tyrannies, his dark suspicions, his morbid fears, his insane hates, and his wild and furious vindictiveness—all point to but one conclusion, that the man is both mentally and morally diseased, to such an extent that he is wholly and totally an unsafe person to be entrusted with the exercise of power. Our people are law-abiding—are patient—are long suffering. They do not desire to have such madmen force them in self-defence to some act of violence, which will forever rid them of this petty scourge. And yet to this complexion must it come at last, if these outrages continue to be put upon them. Human nature cannot bear beyond a certain point. That point is now reached. They will not, nor they cannot stand by and see themselves degraded to brutes. These wrongs cry to Heaven for an avenger, and vengeance will assuredly come and sweep forever from our path these atrocities, as surely as the sun will rise to-morrow, if our patience and our manhood are further trampled upon. Then is something dangerous in the human breast, which let him beware of who trifles with it. The unchained tiger is not more terrible than the bursting forth of the wrath of a people stung to madness. We had better grovel in the dust at once and permit this Gesler of our Switzerland to trample over our prostrate bodies, than to hold our peace when such enormities are committed. These things can go no further. Either they must stop of themselves, or a stop will be found for them. We conclude as we begin. We believe this man is a raving maniac. We believe him a common nuisance—we know him a petty scourge. We are men—with the blood of freemen coursing in our veins, and we had better die at once than see our loved and respected fellow-citizens rotting in a dungeon, because they have striven to protect us from the coward oppressor and dastard despoiler of our common liberties.

[The late hour of going to press Monday night, precluded us more than mentioning the mere fact of the last greatest enormity.]

We call public attention to the following correspondence, that between the imprisoned justices and members of the Waco bar:

IN THE DUNGEON OF THE JAIL, }
Midnight, May 6, 1872. }

To the Members of the Waco Bar:

The undersigned, members of the County Court of McLennan County, being in the jail of said County, by note of the Hon. J. W. Oliver, Judge of the 33d Judicial District, on a charge of being in contempt of said Court for passing the accompanying order of said County Court, do respectfully ask your opinion, whether said order is in the scope of the discretion of said County Court, in the discharge of their duties under the law.

We ask this because we are in jail by order of the said District Court, to remain, and pay a fine of one hundred dollars each per day, until we rescind said order. We passed said order, believing we were protecting the rights of the people, and if right, we will never re-cind said order—if wrong we wish to put ourselves right, and undo what we have done.

We are, gentlemen,
Very respectfully yours,
O. H. LELAND,
J. P. Precinct No. 1.
R. A. DYER,
J. P. Precinct No. 2.
J. J. RIDDLE,
J. P. Precinct No. 4.

WACO, May 7, 1872.

Gentlemen:

In accordance with your written request transmitted to us from the jail, in which you are incarcerated, we have made a careful examination of the law, and are of opinion that the Judge of the District Court has no authority to draw upon the County Treasury for extra services of Sheriff, Clerk, or Bailiff. We think further that the Honorable County Court had the authority to pass the order to which you refer, and that, if, in your judgment such order was necessary to protect the interest of the county, it was your sworn duty to have passed it. The law provides for the compensation of officers and specifies the manner in which their accounts shall be audited and paid. It is our opinion that in the passage of the order, for which you are imprisoned, you were acting on a matter clearly within your discretion under the law, and within the jurisdiction of your Court, and your action, whether right or wrong, was not in contempt of the District Court or the Judge thereof.

We respectfully tender you as honored and respected members of the County Court our sympathy, and in common with all good people of our county, we feel that your incarceration in a dungeon with common felons is one of the most flagrant outrages ever inflicted upon the people of this county. Respectfully,

E. J. Gurley, John T. Flint, Richard Coke, W. M. Flournoy, George Clark, J. T. Dixon, Wm. Lambdin Prather, S. H. Renick, M. D. Herring, E. H. Graham, D. A. Kelley, Thomas Moore, Charles B. Pearre, J. W. Dickinson, F. H. Sleeper, E. A. McKenney, James M. Anderson, W. H. Jenkins, David H. Hewlett, John C. West, Silas C. Buck, N. W. Battle, L. C. Alexander.

Full particulars in this important matter will be published in the Daily ADVANCE to-morrow morning.

Waco newspaper declaring Judge Oliver a lunatic. The date should be May 7, 1872

113

TROUBLES IN THE WACO COURT

The outlawry running rampant in Texas during Reconstruction had the citizenry outraged. The killings in and around Waco, coupled with the theft activities drew much criticism about the inept State Police and the court system. Most Texas lawyers had served in the Confederate army and were bypassed in court appointments by the Carpetbagger regime following the war. Waco was no exception.

Governor Davis, who had won the governorship of Texas in 1869 in an election supervised by the federal military commander, intended to reconstruct the entire state in the image of Republicanism. This provided the ingredients for a collision course with the radical Republican John W. Oliver, who had been appointed by Davis as Judge of the 33rd District Court. Judge Oliver assumed office on January 1, 1870. He presided over the judicial district that embraced McLennan, Limestone and Falls Counties.

The Waco courthouse was located on the square at Second and Franklin streets. It was the second courthouse to adorn the square, having been constructed in 1857-8 at a cost of $11,000. The contract called for a 50 x 60 foot, three-story building, of brick or stone. Floors were to be laid with pine planks, tongue and grooved. A fireproof roof was required, with a spire mounted in the center, 20 feet high, and covered with tin. The availability of rest rooms to the public is not known, but a problem caused the court on May 25, 1867, to levy a five-dollar fine for the offense of "depositing urine anywhere in the courthouse." The sheriff was directed to have lime and sawdust thrown in the corners and under the stairs to destroy the "offensive odors."

Another problem at the Waco courthouse occurred when two men fell out of the doors of the upper rooms and plunged to their deaths. The Police Court on June 4, 1867, noted that banisters had been erected across the doors to prevent the same from happening again. An appropriation of $20 dollars in U.S. currency was approved for the expenditure, the court records noted.

Judge Oliver conducted his court in an arbitrary and distasteful fashion to the lawyers and citizens of the district. A confrontation with the McLennan County Commissioners' Court occurred on April 20, 1872. It culminated with the Commissioners refusing county funds to pay for extra services of the sheriff, district clerk and bailiffs for the District Court authorized by Judge Oliver.

The action by the commissioners incurred the wrath of Judge Oliver who cited the entire Commissioners' Court guilty of contempt. He assessed a fine of $100 dollars a day against each member of the Court, and ordered the entire body to be jailed until the fines were paid. A Grand Jury friendly to Judge Oliver was impaneled on May 1, 1872, and promptly indicted Commissioners O.H. Leland, Robert A. Dyer, J.J. Riddle, John Wood and S. M. Johnson on four counts of embezzlement (Causes 1606-1609), charging them with illegally authorizing the payment of public funds in their official capacities.

The jailing of the commissioners fanned the flames of discontent with the citizens. Feelings soon reached a heated pitch against Judge Oliver and his bailiffs. The Waco Advance newspaper published an "extra" edition on May 7, 1872, citing Judge Oliver as "little better than a raving maniac, and his proper place would be in an insane asylum."

The paper published a letter directed to members of the Waco bar association from the imprisoned commissioners, dated "Midnight, May 6, 1872, from the dungeon of the jail." The letter sought the opinion of the bar members in the dispute with the judge. As expected, the bar members were unanimous in their opinion that the law provided for the salary and expenses of the court personnel and that Judge Oliver had violated the law by seeking more compensation for the officials. The bar members expressed sympathy with the plight of the commissioners, stating their incarceration "in a dungeon with common felons is one of the most flagrant outrages ever inflicted upon the people of this county."

While the entire Commissioners' Court were imprisoned, Edward Gurley, a member of the bar, overheard his brother-in-law, Dr. John Sears, remark that he believed Judge Oliver to be crazy. Gurley requested Dr. Sears to contact the other physicians of McLennan County, and to impanel a lunacy commission to consider the sanity of the Judge. The Lunacy Commission promptly certified to Judge Leland, Chief Justice of the Commissioners Court, that Judge Oliver was, indeed, a lunatic.

The certificate, together with a warrant for Judge Oliver's arrest, was taken to the county jail for Judge Leland's signature. The warrant was quickly signed, then handed to Constable John Moore for execution. While Judge Oliver was away from the bench during lunchtime, Moore arrested him on the courthouse steps. Oliver requested enough time to close his court, but Moore, knowing Oliver's crony, Sheriff W.H. Morris, would intervene, refused and took the judge to the county jail where he was locked up.

This action created a unique situation in that the District Judge and the entire Commissioners' Court, including the Chief Justice and all the Justices of the Peace, were all incarcerated in the county jail at the same time, each faction having been imprisoned by order of the other.

Sheriff Morris and the bailiffs tried several legal maneuvers but were unable to secure the release of the judge. Judge Oliver then recognized the need for compromise and proposed to Gurley that he would order the release of the Commissioners' Court from jail if Gurley would secure the dismissal of the lunacy complaint. Gurley, not trusting Oliver, first required him to sign the release order in his jail cell, which he did.

After all parties were released from jail, Oliver immediately convened his court and launched into a tirade castigating all those who had participated in having him declared a lunatic. Gurley stepped to the bench and informed Oliver that the lunacy charges had not been dismissed and that continuation of the actions by the judge would result in a trip to the insane asylum for him. This sealed the compromise and ended the incident. The indictments against all defendants were dismissed on August 20, 1872.

Judge Oliver's troubles were far from over, however. In 1873, he was arrested and jailed on a charge that he had accepted a bribe to allow 'Tehuacana Bill' Posey to escape from jail. The judge was released on bail furnished by two fellow Republicans, Geo. O'Brien and O.H. Leland, the Chief Justice whom Oliver had ordered sent to jail in May, 1872.

Oliver was never brought to trial on the bribery charge. He died on August 12, 1874, at Waco, of "pulmonary consumption, super-added to which is congestion of the brain." The diagnosis was published in the August 11, 1874, edition of the *Waco Examiner.*

In 1873, Waco lawyer Richard Coke announced his candidacy for the office of governor of the State of Texas opposing the unpopular Davis. This was the same Richard Coke who had defended Bill Posey in the early theft charges. Coke had gained five acquittals for Posey before losing on the two counts of mule theft that resulted in Posey's conviction and prison sentence. Coke had also won a civil judgment against Posey for attorney fees, causing the subsequent sheriff's sale of Posey's land to satisfy the judgment.

Coke was a man of large stature, with a massive bald head, a heavy growth of beard, and a voice that "roared like a bull when angry." He was said never to be without the Bible he carried in his pocket. He was born in Willamsburg, Va., March 13, 1829, the son of John and Eliza Coke. He graduated from William & Mary College in 1849, passed the bar in 1850, and practiced law at Waco with the firm of Coke, Herring and Anderson.

He married Mary Horne of Waco in 1852, and four children were born to them. He enlisted in the Confederate Army as a private and was discharged a captain. He was a district judge, then a judge on the Texas Supreme Court until General Philip Sheridan, commander of the Union forces in Texas following the war, removed him as an "impediment to Reconstruction."

Coke beat the incumbent Davis in the fall election by a huge majority. One of his campaign platforms was to eliminate Davis' State Police Force, which most considered ineffective and oppressive. Coke was inaugurated in January 1874, but Davis refused to give up office. He fortified himself with his Negro state police guards on the first floor of the capitol and wired President U.S. Grant to send reinforcements to back him.

Governor-elect Coke and the newly elected legislature maintained their position on the second floor of the capitol, and Texas operated under a dual governorship for a time. President Grant finally refused to intervene, and Davis and his guards were forced to vacate the capitol. The defeat was an extremely bitter pill for Davis. He remained as a leader of the republicans in Texas until his death in 1883.

The election of Coke was like the dawning of a new light following the dark days of Reconstruction that shrouded Texas. Coke and the new legislature quickly abolished the State Police and ushered in the strengthened Texas Rangers. Texas citizens cheered the election and the new regime. The new administration ended Radical Rule and restored government to the people.

Many problems lay ahead for Coke and post-war Texas-- Indian raids on the frontier, continued Mexican forays, subsidy decisions and routes for the emerging railroad network--but at least Texas now had a governor that his own man, and there was jubilation.

Bill Posey was still on the loose and reportedly still causing havoc among the farmers and ranchers over a wide area of central Texas. The Texas press reported Posey's gang was stealing horses, mules and cattle in broad open daylight. It was said the gang would ride up to a ranch, round up a herd, and drive it off, the owners powerless to stop the brazen thieves.

Things were still too hot for Posey and his men in McLennan County, so they shifted their activities south to the areas of San Antonio and New Braunfels. They would then drive their stolen herds into Indian Territory. Texas was full of badmen at the time, but Posey's name struck fear in the hearts of the citizens. Streets were cleared whenever it was whispered that Posey and his men were in the area.

The *Galveston News* reported the Posey gang, after selling a herd of livestock, rode into the little German town of New Braunfels to celebrate their latest windfall. Dismounting, they tied their horses to the saloon hitching rail, strode inside and ordered the bartender to bring whiskey. After a few drinks, some of the outlaws decided to partake of another kind of celebration, mounted their horses and proceeded to shoot up the town.

They thundered through the little town yelling like wild Comanches, firing their pistols in the air and terrorizing the community. They promptly drove all the people indoors and closed every business in town except the saloon, which Posey forced the terrified proprietor to keep open. The outlaws, the paper said, stopped long enough to reenter the saloon, down a few more drinks and be off again on their wild tirade.

The Comal County sheriff was reported to be a cool and fearless man, but he was able to calculate the insurmountable odds in attempting a one-man challenge to the outlaws. He set about seeking assistance from some of the towns' citizens in putting down the desperadoes. He finally persuaded some fifteen men to take up arms and follow him to the saloon. Armed with shotguns, muskets, pistols and rifles, they headed from the courthouse to the watering hole where the gang was imbibing for the next foray through town. One of the outlaws spotted the approaching citizen-posse and shouted a warning that the law was coming. The desperadoes waited with drawn guns.

When the posse reached the saloon, the sheriff ordered them to charge inside, which they did. Their courage soon melted when the outlaws sprang forward to meet the challenge. The sheriff, however, was forced to play his hand. With six-shooter drawn, he quickly pulled the trigger, and one outlaw dropped with a bullet to the heart. Two outlaws fired at the same instant, and the sheriff went down with two bullet holes to the breast gushing blood.

The posse now disappeared, but the outlaws knew it was time to abandon the tirade they had launched in the little community. After one last drink, they rushed to the waiting horses, fired their weapons in the air and roared out of town yelling and whooping wildly. Posey and seven of his followers spurred their mounts into the Hill Country, camping out along the way at Marble Falls, a favorite outlaw hideout.

In a couple of days the band rode into Lampasas, where they intended to "stir things up" as they had done in New Braunfels. But a couple of Texas Rangers happened to be in town and was visiting with the sheriff when the outlaws appeared. The sound of gunfire brought the Rangers and the sheriff outside to investigate the commotion. The sheriff immediately recognized Posey, and with the Rangers at his side, advanced on the intruders.

A brisk skirmish ensued, resulting in superficial wounds to Posey and one of his men when the sheriff and Rangers unleashed a fusillade of return fire. The outlaws made a mad dash out of town, but the lawmen were hot on their heels. Posey, an excellent judge of horseflesh, always made sure his men were atop the best and swiftest horses that could be found. They outdistanced their pursuers, who continued the chase firing at the vanishing outlaws.

The *Galveston News* reported a member of the gang, a man named Taylor, was superbly mounted on a superior animal with great speed. He began lagging behind the others, it said, taunting the sheriff and the Rangers, just keeping out of range of their rifles. Sometimes he would dismount and fire at the advancing lawmen until their bullets began to sing by his ears. He would then remount and ride away, yelling defiance. Taylor repeated the act several times and escaped unscathed. Finally a Ranger named Frank Tower grew tired of the outlaw's bravado and decided the next time it happened he would respond with a special challenge.

Tower, it was reported, carried an old, single-shot .50 caliber buffalo rifle, which he retrieved from the scabbard beneath the saddle fender while his horse was on the run. The outlaw Taylor dismounted again and fired at the lawmen. Tower pulled his horse to an abrupt halt, leaped from the animal and laid the barrel of the old buffalo gun in the fork of a mesquite bush. Taking careful aim, he squeezed the trigger, and the roar could be heard for miles. The shot struck the surprised Taylor in the breast. He jumped up with his hands over his head and fell back on the ground with a moan, mortally wounded, the newspaper reported.

As the Rangers and the sheriff rode up to him, Taylor raised himself up and pulled off one boot. Gasping for breath, he begged a Ranger to help him pull off the other boot. The Ranger stepped forward to help him, but with one last groan Taylor fell back dead. Posey and the other outlaws made good their escape. None of their bullets had struck the Rangers or the sheriff. The officers tied the dead body of Taylor on his horse and headed their mounts back to Lampasas.

The wounded Posey made his way to the sanctuary of his father's home at Horn Hill, in Limestone County. There he could recover and plot his next move. The Posey homestead was well guarded by a sentry of guineas and geese who would gabble a constant alarm at the approach of a human stranger. L o c a l authorities had word that Posey was back in the area and attempted to slip up on the ranch and nab him. When word spread to Posey that lawmen were on their way, or when the alert was sounded by the flock of fowls, he slipped out of the house and made good his escape into the "Posey Thicket," where no lawman dared to tread.

Posey next surfaced in McLennan County, it was reported, driving a herd of stolen horses ahead of him. He had taken the horses in broad daylight from the ranch of a German in Hill County. He was quickly recognized, and word got to the sheriff that Posey was again in the area. The sheriff dispatched a posse and started after him. He was cornered in the Brazos River bottom just a few miles from his home and Waco. A spirited gun battle ensued, but Posey was able to slip by the posse. This time he headed for the Indian Territory and sanctuary among friends and family.

Another tragedy came to Louisa Aikman with the apparent death of her third husband, Albert Aikman. Knowing the lands on Tehuacana Creek would be lost because of the lawsuits, Aikman had bought a larger farm in Comanche County. There he would move Louisa and their two sons, plus the widow, Sarah Ann Wallace, and her two children. All were now living on the Hensley survey since the lynching of Matt Wallace.

Aikman was preparing to leave and inspect the land to the west he had just purchased. The Indian threat west of the Brazos River was still a reality, but activities had subsided somewhat in recent years. He had been warned not to take the chance by traveling alone, but decided he would be safe with the proper armament. He left the farm astride his favorite saddle horse. A packhorse loaded with needed provisions followed behind.

Two days after Aikman left the homestead his packhorse returned with several Indian arrows imbedded in the packs. An ex-Ranger identified the arrows as Comanche. Aikman was never heard from again. Louisa had now been widowed three times. Each husband's death had come at a time when his children were very young. None of the children ever knew their father.

The tragedies on the Tehuacana had caused great sadness. A grieving Elizabeth Posey waited with her three sons at the Posey home, distraught and heart-broken at the events that had shattered their lives.

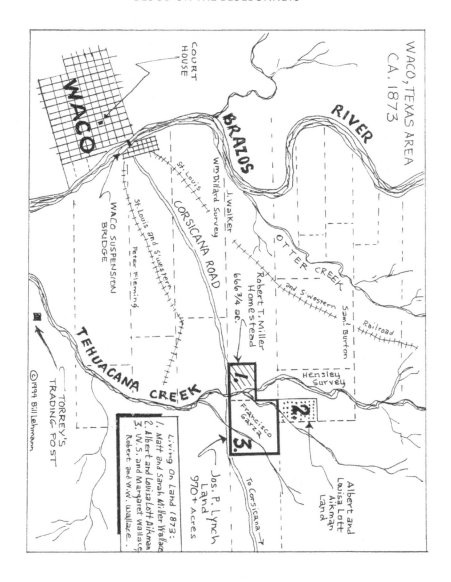

WACO, TEXAS AREA
CA. 1873

BRAZOS RIVER

COURT HOUSE

WACO

WACO SUSPENSION BRIDGE

St. Louis

St. Louis and S. western

Peter Fleming

Wm. Dillard Survey

J. Walker

CORSICANA ROAD

OTTER CREEK

Robert T. Miller Homestead
666 3/4 ac.

2nd S. western

Sam'l Burton

Railroad

Hensley Survey

Francisco Garza

Albert and Louisa Lott Aikman Land

TEHUACANA CREEK

© 1994 Bill Lehmann

TORREY'S TRADING POST

1.

2.

3.

To Corsicana →

Jos. P. Lynch Land
970+ Acres

Living On Land 1873:
1. Matt and Sarah Miller Wallace
2. Albert and Louisa Lott Aikman
3. W.S. and Margaret Wallace,
Robert and W.W. Wallace.

CAPTURE AND ESCAPE OF BILL POSEY

After making his way across the Red River and into Indian Territory, Posey reined his horse north to the Creek Nation. There he had many kinfolk who had settled along the Arkansas River after the forced removal from their former homes in Alabama. He had met these relatives during his term of service in the Confederate cavalry when the Texans had been sent to the Creek Nation and Indian Territory.

Posey, being one-half Creek Indian, qualified as a citizen of the Nation. He could select land anywhere he wanted to settle because the Indians did not believe in individual land ownership. All tribal members owned the land, and they could build anything or anywhere they wanted. Posey built a cabin on Cane Creek, midway between the small Creek settlements of Muskogee and Okmulgee, but the long arm of the law was about to reach into Indian Territory and snatch him back to Texas and the prison term he had so far avoided.

Texas authorities had been alerted Posey was living on Cane Creek. On June 29, 1874, Texas officers from Sherman consisted of J.L. Hall, Bill Everheart, S.D. Ball and Burt Douglass. They arrived the Sunday before within five miles of the ranch of Posey, and halted for the night due to a severe storm. Just at daybreak on Monday, they started and in a short time came in sight of the ranch.

They discovered Posey starting out on the prairie in search of his horses. The officers divided, and a part secured position in the stables or lots. Two of the men started out to watch his movements. He shortly returned to the house and Posey proceeded to the stable where the officers stepped out with guns drawn and ordered him to surrender, which he did, though reluctantly. The lawmen left at once with the prisoner for Muskogee. There they boarded a train, transporting the prisoner back to Texas.

An article in the *Denison Herald* of July 14, 1874, reported that deputy sheriff Hall "had returned from Muskogee, in the Nation, where he had put the cuffs on W.A.J. Posey, mule thief and fratricide."

Leigh (Lee) Hall would become famous as a Texas Ranger, but in 1874 he was serving as a deputy sheriff out of Grayson County, based in the town of Denison. He was born October 8, 1849, at Lexington, North Carolina. His father was a surgeon and his grandfather a minister. He first came to Grayson County as a schoolmaster before being appointed a City Marshal at Sherman in 1871. He had since been appointed a deputy sheriff. Most people called him "Red" because of his flaming red hair that could be seen for a long distance. He was considered "intelligent, shrewd, sociable, and possessed of extraordinary qualifications for the detection and arrest of the criminal element."

Thus Posey was captured in the Creek Nation and returned to Texas. Hall transported Posey back to McLennan County, where he was lodged in jail to await formal sentencing on the mule theft charge. He retained new attorneys who requested a new trial, and he awaited court action. The hearing finally came, but the decision was not favorable. A news article in the *Waco Examiner* dated Friday, July 29, 1874, stated: "Bill Posey was taken into court yesterday morning. The application for a new trial was overruled and sentence passed. The officers started for the depot, but found the train had left. He was then placed in jail and will go down. Five years in the penitentiary is the sentence."

Posey began his five-year sentence at hard labor, but the conditions of the prison were so repulsive and oppressive that Posey became incorrigible. So wild were his antics that he had to be constantly restrained and placed in solitary confinement. It was reported that guards were constantly dousing him with water to keep him subdued.

The 1874 prison system in Texas was plagued with many detrimental conditions. County sheriffs and deputies were charged with escorting prisoners to the state penitentiary at Huntsville, and the convicts were forced to work in various shops and factories housed within the institution. A recommendation passed during the Reconstruction Convention in 1871, allowed prisoners to be leased out to private individuals for labor.

These men, known as lessees, paid the state for the convict labor and use of the facilities, and more or less managed the system. The lessee paid a prisoner clothing allowance, fed the convicts, and furnished payroll for the guards. The state kept an inspector on the site to observe the prison operations and report to the Governor.

In addition to the use of convicts in and around the prison, the prisoners were hired out to large labor employers, mainly road contractors and railroad companies. Brutalities to the convicts, especially those in labor camps, had increased significantly during this period. Other problems with the lessee system included an increase in escapes, and less concern with the personal hygiene of the prisoner or sanitation of the prison. This resulted in a large increase in sickness and death among the prison population.

Posey served 20 months of personal prison torture, and every day he plotted his escape. He was one day working on a chain gang, supervised by five armed guards, when he spotted his chance for freedom. A *Chicago Times* article described the events:

"While working (on the chain gang) one day with a 12 pound ball attached to his leg, Posey watched his chance. He struck down one of his guards with a stone, and stood off four more of the guard. He called out to the prison authorities to come and re-arrest him and he would kill them all for their cruel treatment.

"Holding all the dodigidy officers at bay, he slowly retreated towards some horses grazing nearby. Getting a horse between him and the guards, he cooly picked up the ball, slung it over the horse, mounted the animal and rode off to the safety of his father's home. There he secured tools with which he obtained freedom from the shackles. He also secured his own guns, revolver, a good horse, and crossed the Red River, and back into Indian Territory."

The tragedy of events was too much for Elizabeth Posey to handle. She died in 1875 at the age of 27 of what family members described as a broken heart. The events had been unkind to the families. They were now estranged. They had lost their land, and

Elizabeth's brother, Matt, had been murdered, many said at the hands of his own brother-in-law, Bill Posey.

Elizabeth left behind three young sons: Matthew Andrew, 9; Albert Washington, 8, and Robert, age 3. With the death of Elizabeth, the boys went to live with their grandparents, Washington and Margaret Wallace, who were still living on the Lynch portion of the Garza survey lands.

Learning of the death of Elizabeth, Posey dispatched an ally and family friend to go to McLennan County to fetch his sons. The friend told Wallace that Posey was prepared to "come back and kill you all" if his order was denied. The boys were sent.

Changes had taken place in Texas and Indian Territory with the connection of rail service. The first train into Texas from the north chugged into Denison, via a new bridge across the Red River, in 1874. It would now be a fast trip from Dallas to Muskogee on the *Katy Flyer*, of the Missouri, Kansas and Texas railroad.

The Posey boys were last seen by family members as the train pulled away from the Waco depot bound for Dallas. There they would board the *Flyer* and travel to Indian Territory.

The heads of the Posey boys protruded from the windows of the train, their hair blowing in the breeze, and catching cinders from the smokestack of the moving train as it puffed north to the reunion with their father, Texas outlaw Bill Posey.

A NEW LIFE AND CULTURE
IN INDIAN TERRITORY

Bill Posey's father, Benjamin Franklin Posey, was born in Troup County, Georgia in 1806. Benjamin married his first cousin, Eliza Berryhill, December 20, 1834, in Georgia. Family members said the couple eloped because it was against Creek tribal law for first cousins to marry. Somehow they escaped the usual tribal punishment for the offense, and settled in Chambers County, Alabama. Benjamin was one-half Creek through his mother, Nancy Berryhill, a full blood. Eliza was one-half Creek through her father, Thomas S. Berryhill, a brother to Benjamin's mother.

Intermarriage between the Indians and the early white settlers in North America was commonplace. The Creeks, as well as other Native American tribes, had accepted the Pilgrims and their offspring, and many mixed marriages had occurred, and they lived in a relatively peaceful existence unless incited by outside influences.

The Creeks, like their brethren, the Cherokees, Choctaws, Seminoles and Chickasaws, had relinquished some of their lands through treaties, but the settlers always wanted more, each time pushing the Indians farther west. The government, listening to the clamor of the settlers, adopted a policy of removal of these tribes to an area west of the Mississippi River. The Indians had lived in relative peace with the white invaders, but as more arrived, skirmishes ensued between the two groups, resulting in the Creek War and the serious effort to relocate the tribes.

Some Creeks wanted to relocate. Other factions of the tribe wanted no part of removal and vowed to fight to the bitter end to retain their homeland. General William McIntosh, a leader of the Lower Creek faction, believed removal was the only realistic solution to the problems of his people, but he encouraged the Creek Council in passing a tribal law in 1823 providing for the death penalty for any Creek ceding land without the approval of the Council.

In 1824, federal commissioners assembled some advocates of voluntary removal to a meeting in Coweta. For reasons yet unknown, McIntosh and most of the other Creek leaders at the meeting agreed to cede the remnants of the Creek lands in Georgia and part of the Alabama lands for lands in the Indian Territory. McIntosh, in so doing, had violated the Council law and must pay the penalty. The Council directed Menawa, one of the conservative chiefs opposed to removal, to assassinate McIntosh.

With a force of some one hundred men of the Okfuskee tribe, Menawa arrived at the home of Principal Chief McIntosh just before dawn on the morning of May 1, 1825. Several guests, including some white men, were in the house. Menawa's men surrounded the house and called to the guests and the women and children to leave. Only McIntosh and Etommee Tustennuggee, another signer, remained in the house. The Okfuskees set fire to the house, and when the two occupants ran from the blazing structure, Menawa and his men cut them down. They then destroyed the cattle and other property of the dead chief, which was tribal custom.

Following the assassination of their chief, the McIntosh faction reached an agreement with the federal government to relocate. An advance group was sent out to look at the new lands in Indian Territory. The first party of lower Creeks arrived at Fort Gibson, the processing center, in 1828. Numbering about 1,300, they settled in the valley of the Arkansas River, just west of the new lands that had been set-aside for the Cherokees.

The Upper Creek faction attempted to remain in their homeland as agreed to in the new treaties, but a group called the "Red Sticks," in frustration, lashed out at the white man's world. Roving bands killed white settlers, destroying their cabins, livestock, barns and crops. White refugees streamed into Columbus, Georgia, as the so-called Creek War broke out. General Andrew Jackson conducted a successful war against the Creeks. A young lieutenant, Sam Houston, who exhibited bravery in the campaign, even though wounded severely twice, aided him. Both men would have a future impact on the events of Texas and the Indian Territory.

The defeat of the Creeks forced the tribe over the removal trail and to the new homeland. More than 14,000 Creeks began the journey to Indian Territory in 1836 and 1837. Most arrived at Fort Gibson in absolutely wretched condition. The Eastern Cherokee tribe had the same experience. In the winter of 1838-39 the last pitiful band of Eastern Cherokees arrived in the Indian Territory. Their suffering had made even the soldiers who had been sent to carry out the forced removal to weep for their unfortunate Indian charges.

The government had made arrangements with so-called "contractors" to assist in moving the families, but the contractors left most of their baggage and supplies behind. Critics called the removal nothing more than genocide, for the removal came in the dead of winter. The Indians were poorly clothed, and supplies had been left behind, many said purposefully. The trip of 1,200 miles had taken more than three months to complete. More than 3,500 Creeks had been buried along the removal trail. Conservative estimates claim perhaps forty percent of the Creek population was lost during and immediately after the removal.

Arriving at Fort Gibson, the Creeks found the supplies of blankets, food provisions and farm implements had not been waiting for them on arrival as promised. It would be another four years before the government would send the needed supplies, and then in short measure, adding more credence to the charges of attempted genocide by the government. Investigation revealed that most of the contractors were unscrupulous friends and relatives of the government officials and politicians. Other tribes in the forced removal would have the same experience.

Life was extremely difficult for the new arrivals, which had no livestock and few tools. The Lower Creeks settled in the northern part of the new land, along the Arkansas and Verdigris Rivers. This group included the Poseys, Berryhills, Harjos and Smiths, who were all related. The Upper Creeks spread out along the Deep

Fork, North Canadian and Canadian Rivers, in the southern part of the new Creek Nation. The Indians named their new settlements after their old towns they had left behind in an attempt to preserve as much of their old society as possible.

In time, the Creeks, who had been extremely adept at farming and stockraising, began slowly building their herds. Some had brought seeds, which they planted, and crops of corn, squash, pumpkins and beans once again became a part of the diet. They had existed on an abundance of wild game in the territory, including elk, deer, bear, wild turkey, quail, rabbit and squirrel.

As their bounty increased, they found their Plains Indian neighbors to the west venturing into their settlements stealing horses and cattle. They even murdered a few of the Indian settlers, as they did their white adversaries in Texas. The Creeks called these Indians, the Kiowa and Comanche, the "wild tribes." There was also trouble with the Osages to the north, who had been relocated from their tribal lands in Missouri and Kansas.

The Five Civilized Tribes were basically a cultured people, and not much different from their white counterparts. In many cases, the Indians were better educated than the settlers. A Cherokee, Sequoyah, had invented the Cherokee alphabet, and even before removal the Indians were reading their own newspapers published on presses in their original homeland. Many of the white settlers could neither read nor write. The Creeks even had their own newspaper, The Indian Journal, published in English in the new town of Eufaula after relocating.

Most Native Americans, including the Creeks, did not believe in individual ownership of the land. They were merely caretakers under tribal ownership. They could locate their home wherever they chose. They kept their log homes neat, and there was always a cast-iron kettle of *sofky,* (hominy), at the fireplace. They had tribal laws and town laws, and they had their own police force, called the Lighthorse.

The Principal Chief and the Second Chief of both the Upper and Lower Creek factions were elected for four-year terms. The

Nation was divided into six judicial districts with judges chosen by the National Council. The people in each district through election chose the Lighthorse.

A criminal code was enacted through the National Council, providing for penalties of whipping, branding, or death, according to the severity of the crime. The tribe had no jails. When the Lighthorse arrested a man, he was chained to a tree or another stationary object to await trial, never more than a day or two away. If found guilty, the accused might be whipped or branded on the spot. A man convicted of a capital crime, however, was often released on his own word to prepare for death.

Prior to the execution of a man named Satanoke for murder in 1879, a large group assembled with the condemned, the judge and the execution squad, to hear a sermon. At the appointed time, Satanoke examined and approved his coffin, selected rifles instead of shotguns for the execution, and removed his boots. A lighthorseman would then blindfold the convicted. The captain of the Lighthorse gave the command and the shots fired by the executioners found their mark.

At the time of removal, the Indians and mixed bloods of the Creek tribe had to make a fateful decision as to where they would relocate. Most chose to be relocated with the tribe in Indian Territory. Some, like the Berryhills and Posey, chose a path in both directions. Benjamin Posey, Eliza and the children, which now numbered fourteen, decided to seek their fortune in the new state of Texas. They located in Nacogdoches in 1847, where their fifteenth child was born, before moving on to Horn Hill, in Limestone County. This is where Bill Posey grew up and perfected his skills as a cowboy.

The Civil War plunged Posey into the Indian Territory, where he became familiar with the country and became acquainted with his Posey, Berryhill, Harjo and Smith cousins. Following the War, Posey went back into Texas, married Elizabeth Wallace in 1865, and started a family and a stock raising operation before his troubles with the law.

The white man's Civil War inflicted severe hardships on the Indians living in the Territory. In early 1861, even before Confederate troops fired on Fort Sumpter, the federal government abandoned its posts in Indian Territory, virtually recognizing that the Territory was a part of the South. The government had even cut off the meager subsistence support to the tribes, which also opened influences of the Confederate government. The Choctaws and Chickasaws quickly aligned themselves with the South, but the Creeks, Cherokees and Seminoles were divided over the issue. When the war began, confederate troops from Arkansas and Texas poured in to occupy the abandoned army posts in the Territory. A few battles were fought pitting Indian brother against Indian brother.

Following the war, the Creeks were faced with almost a new beginning. Some members of the tribe had fled north into Kansas during the conflict, and many of the Confederate group of all tribes fled to Texas to avoid the violence of civil strife. When they returned, they found their homes burned, their cattle either missing or their bones bleaching, and their fields overgrown with weeds. A bigger price to pay for the tribe would come with the loss of more land.

The war proved to be a convenient excuse for the federal government to take back lands, which had been granted under the old treaties. Claiming violation of the old treaties by the tribes during the war, the government said new treaties would have to be drawn up, each time resulting in the loss of more land to the tribes. Although the government did not make land reparations against the former confederate states, it did not hesitate to take Indian land.

The western part of the Creek Nation was chopped off, some 3,250,000 acres of it, for which the government paid a paltry thirty cents an acre. The Seminoles were forced to give up their entire region for fifteen cents an acre. The government then sold a small portion of the land on the Creeks' western borders to the Seminoles for fifty cents an acre. The Choctaws and Chickasaws suffered the least. They had to give up their "leased district," which the government had already been leasing since 1855.

Rebuilding was slow following the war, but gradually their herds and farms began improving again. The war had brought new problems with new encroachment by white settlers who were moving out of the eastern United States in larger than ever numbers. The soldiers garrisoned at Fort Gibson prior to the war had regularly put the intruders out, but now that the war was over the soldiers were gone, and there was no police authority to keep out the unwelcome element that was surfacing in the Territory.

The war also produced a sorry criminal element that sought refuge in the Territory. It was becoming a haven for the outlaw and a sanctuary from the long arm of the law in adjoining states, which had no power or inclination to pursue the criminal element after they crossed the territorial border. The outlaw bands would rob, pillage and murder in Texas, Arkansas and Kansas then flee to the Territory where there were numerous hideouts in the hills and caves. And the herds of the Indian were falling prey to the rustlers, who were driving them north to Kansas markets.

Thugs and murderers of all descriptions and notoriety were lurking along the old Texas Road that crossed the Territory from the Missouri border, running southwest to the Red river. The newly installed Butterfield Stage route over the road was drawing attention by the robbers and highwaymen. It was not safe to travel except in numbers and with plenty of armament. The Indian Journal at Eufaula regularly reported the finding of dead bodies along the route, which had been robbed of all their possessions, including identification.

This was the same road that had been hacked out by the army troops in establishing military passage between forts in the early years of the Territory. It was the same road that carried Sam Houston to his famous destiny in Texas after spending four years among the Cherokees at Fort Gibson from 1829-1833. It was the same route traveled by the first longhorn herds from Texas to Missouri in 1844 before quarantines halted the activity.

Bill Posey used the Texas Road extensively in driving his stolen Texas steers to Coffeyville after he became known at checkpoints to the Chisholm Trail. He knew the road well. He was half-Creek. He had friends and relatives in the Territory. He now had his three sons with him in his exile from the Texas law. He was safe from the Texas law for the time being--but things were about to change.

THE BEGINNING OF THE END

Posey might have remained safe in the Territory had he stayed out of Texas. But he kept making forays back across the Red River stealing horses and cattle, bringing the herds back to the Territory and to the subsequent Kansas markets. His notoriety in Texas was widespread now, but he remained one step ahead of the law.

He enlarged his home on Cane Creek where he and his three boys and a new wife, Susan, enjoyed family life. He planted beans, corn, squash and the other crops most raised. He kept hogs and chickens, and supplemented the family meat supply with the abundant wild game. Always mindful of his wanted status in Texas, he added a second story to their home, permitting a wide view of the countryside and observation of approaching visitors. The family regularly went into town purchasing supplies, attending church services and other ordinary family activities. In the winter of 1877, Susan presented the family with another son, Henry.

Meanwhile, back in Texas, Richard Coke had served a two-year term as Governor and was up for re-election in 1876. He won a second term handily but resigned shortly thereafter to take a seat in the United States Senate, which had become vacant. His Lieutenant Governor, Richard B. Hubbard, succeeded Coke.

Hubbard was no ordinary man, and his administration was far from ordinary. He was the biggest and loudest governor Texas ever had. He weighed over four hundred pounds, and it was said his voice could be heard for miles. He carried his bulk well, and he was an extremely impressive man, commanding respect from all with whom he came in contact.

Hubbard was born in Walton County, Georgia, on November 1, 1832. He graduated from Mercer College and Harvard Law School, and practiced law in Tyler, Texas. President Buchanan appointed him United States District Attorney for the Western District of Texas in 1858. He later served in the State Legislature, and during the Civil War commanded the 22nd Regiment of cavalry as a colonel.

Coke had made tremendous strides in returning some order to Texas following the savage years of Reconstruction, but the job was far from finished. The Civil War had gotten many of the soldiers into the habit of shooting their neighbors in a way that many considered proper and just. Thus Hubbard inherited a problem that had not been solved.

Had he left well enough alone, some thought, these fellows might dispose of one another with their own lead, but Hubbard was concerned with law and order conducted properly. He attempted to have local authorities maintain peace in their respective counties, but the chief result was getting more deputies killed. The situation was more serious than he thought, and he pledged increased activities for his Texas Rangers.

Posey's continued antics in Texas were apparently troublesome to an extent that Hubbard wanted an end to it. Perhaps the authorities were still chagrined over his prison escape and defiance of state prison officials. Perhaps some of the Waco citizens who were threatened by the outlaw would not sleep well until he was caught. Perhaps Coke, who knew Posey personally, and had his own unpleasant encounters with the fugitive, influenced Hubbard. The theft of two mules and a five-year prison sentence hardly seemed worth the effort, or expense, to bring Posey back to Texas. For whatever reason, Hubbard finally decided to place a new reward on the head of Posey-dead or alive.

Governor Hubbard petitioned Principal Chief Ward Coachman of the Creek Nation to apprehend Posey and return him to Texas authorities. The petition from Hubbard, dated March 27, 1877, read:

"To the Superintendent or Chief Executive Officer of the Indian Territory: Whereas, it appears by the annexed documents, which are hereby certified to be authentic, that W.A. Posey stands charged with the crime of 'Theft' committed in the State of Texas, and information having been received that the said W.A. Posey has fled from justice and has taken refuge in the Indian Territory.

The Texas Governors and the Creek Chief

Edmund J. Davis
1870-1874

Unpopular
Reconstruction
Governor

Richard B. Coke
1874-1876

Posey's defense lawyer
and later U.S. Senator

Principal Chief Ward Coachman
of the Creek Nation, Indian Territory

The popular Creek Nation chief
ordered the Creek Lighthorse to
being in Pocey dead or aliv on
the orders of Texas authoritiees
for the arrest of Texas outlaw Bill
Posey. Posey also had an arrest
warrant from Judge Parker's
court in Fort Smith, Arkansas for
cattle theft in Indidan Territory

Richard B. Hubbard
1876-1879

Hubbard was Texas' largest governor.
He stood six foot five inches tall and
weighed more than 400 pounds. His
booming voice could be heard all over
the state capitol. Ordered an increase in
the reward on the head of Bill Posey.

*Texas Governor portraits from the Texas
State Governors collection, Austin, Texas.
Portrait of Creek Chief Ward Cooachman
from Oklahoma Historical Society archives
collection, Oklahoma City, Oklahoma.*

"Now, therefore, I, R.B. Hubbard, Governor of the State of Texas, have thought proper, in pursuance of the provisions of the Constitution and laws of the United States, to demand the surrender of W.A. Posey, as a fugitive from justice, and that he be delivered to Daniel Childers, who is hereby appointed the Agent on the part of the State of Texas to receive him.

"Given under my hand, and the Great Seal of the State affixed, at the city of Austin, this 27th day of March, A.D. One Thousand Eight Hundred and Seventy Seven, and of the Independence of the United States One Hundred First and of Texas the Forty Second year. R.B. Hubbard, Governor."

Included in the petition to Chief Coachman were certified copies of the McLennan County Court documents showing the conviction of Posey on the charge of theft of two mules, Cause No. 1436.

Chief Coachman received the requisition from Governor Hubbard and issued the following dispatch to the Creek Lighthorse:

"Whereas it appears from documents placed in my hand as to the crimes committed by W.A. Posey now in the jurisdiction of the Creek Nation and a demand having been made in accordance with the law and truly by R.B. Hubbard, Governor of the State of Texas to receive him. Now therefore, I, Ward Coachman, Principal Chief of the Creek Nation do issue to any lawful officer, Greeting: You are hereby commanded in the name of the Creek Nation to arrest said W.A. Posey and deliver him safely to said David Childers-- herein fail not as the law directs. Given under my hand and seal of the office the day and year above written, Ward Coachman, Principal Chief."

Coachman summoned Suntharlpee, a Lighthorse captain of the Uchee Town district to affect the arrest of Posey, who was known to be a resident of the district. Coachman instructed the captain to select two of his best men to assist in the arrest. They knew Posey, and they knew his arrest was going to be a difficult task.

Chief Ward Coachman was a pleasant and popular leader of

the Creeks. He was born in Wetumka, Alabama, in 1827, and went to neighboring schools in Macon County. He was the youngest son of Mushlushobie (who adopted the Christianized name of Coachman), a full-blood Creek. His mother was Pollie Durant, who was a one-half Creek.

Coachman lived with his uncle Loughlin Durant until he was 22 years of age, when he went to the Indian Territory on a scouting mission. Finding the new country favorable, he returned to Alabama and began making preparations to move some remaining Creeks to the new country. A party of 65 Creeks arrived in the new country six weeks later, guided by Coachman.

Coachman became a trader among the so-called "wild tribes" to the west, but a band of Caddoes returning from a hunt carried off some of his stock. He was nearly killed but managed to make it back home. He then entered retail business near his home in Wetumka, I.T., and was involved in agriculture until the Civil War broke out. He served in the Confederate army under Col. Chilly McIntosh as a lieutenant. At the close of the war, he became a leader among the Creeks and was elected Chief in 1875.

Duties of the Creek Lighthorse as defined by the Creek General Council in the Uniform Code adopted for the Nation in 1840, were to "destroy all spirituous liquors brought into the Nation, and inflict penalty and levy a fine upon all persons found guilty of introducing it, or commission of other offenses." The code also mentioned the Lighthorse should monitor the "ever-present cattle herders who passed through the Nation on their way to the Northern markets, and to watch for lawless bands who roamed the Territory."

A Lighthorse company consisted of a captain and three or four privates. Their compensation was four hundred dollars per year for the captain, and half that for the privates. The people in their respective districts elected them for a term of two years. The Lighthorse were furnished guns and ammunition in order to carry out their duties. There was no official uniform, but they were supplied with a badge for identification purposes. The Daniel

Childers named in the documents by Gov. Hubbard as being authorized to receive Posey for the State of Texas, was a captain of the Creek Lighthorse.

Following the removal of the soldiers at Fort Gibson, the Lighthorse provided the only law enforcement in the Territory. They were poorly equipped and not enough in number to adequately provide protection. Murder was commonplace and the number of unsavory characters traveling through the Territory was growing because of inadequate law enforcement. Life was cheap in the 1870's in Indian Territory.

Creek Lighthorseman

Some said there were no Sundays (a day of rest) west of St. Louis, and no God west of Fort Smith.

The government had seated Judge Isaac Parker on the bench of the federal court at Fort Smith in 1875. His jurisdiction was to include the Indian Territory in an effort to stem the lawless tide. In his first court term Parker sentenced eight men to be hanged. This was carried out with great public ceremony on gallows erected next to the federal courthouse in Fort Smith. He quickly gained the title of "Hanging Judge Parker," and his system of justice was carried out 88 times in the twenty years he presided over the court.

Those two decades also saw 65 of his deputies killed in the line of duty in attempting arrests of the lawless breed inhabiting western Arkansas and Indian Territory. Some said the record showed both a persistence of his efforts in effecting a death penalty for major crimes, but the lack of success in bringing law and order to the region. The government, the courts or local authorities were never able to contain a population that included renegade white and black outlaws and Indians of every conceivable blood mix that preyed on the Territory. The same record could be applied as well to the state of Texas during this period.

The Chicago Times, who kept a correspondent at Fort Smith and regularly reported news of the Territory, (mostly the bad news), reported Judge Parker had dispatched two deputy U.S. Marshals to the Territory in an effort to take Posey into custody. The times reported that deputies approached Posey's home on Cane Creek, midway between Muskogee and Okmulgee, and attempted his arrest. Posey, the article said, agreed to accompany them to Fort Smith, but invited the deputies into the house for dinner before they left on the 75mile trip. He placed chairs at the table and was making preparations to leave, "but he suddenly reached in under his couch, brought out his six-shooter and sent one ball through the thigh of one deputy and another through the eye of the other, and drove them from the house.

"He ordered them to throw up their hands, and then cooly asked for the writ (arrest order). This he destroyed and compelled the outwitted and conquered officers to go in and partake of the meal prepared for them, and let them go back to report their failure."

Posey continued his operations out of the Territory for some 15 months after his escape from the Texas penitentiary. He and his family moved openly in the Territory, where they were well received. He participated in the fall and spring roundups with other stockmen in the area, never seeking to throw a "sticky loop" over any of his neighbors' livestock. Cattle ran the open range and the estray law prevailed during this period before the invention and use of barbed wire, which fenced off the owners' property. Life and activity of the times regarding the estray law may be found in the pages of the *Indian Journal*, published at Eufaula, I.T.:

"ROUNDING UP ESTRAYS. With each recurring spring comes the gathering of horsemen and rounding up, or surrounding a large tract of country, and all approaching a common center, driving before them with a merry shout and loud halloos, the cracking of whips and hard riding, all the unbranded and estray cattle within the circle. They often come from many miles to seek their own. This year they all met at the rock quarry, where a field enclosed with a stone fence will hold the wildest steer. Nearly one hundred men had gathered nearly fifty head. The owners selected all that could be identified, branded them and drove them back to their range.

"The estrays will be advertised for six months and sold if unclaimed. Many of the cattle roaming on the broad prairie will wander twenty miles or more from home. After they get wonted to a range they seldom leave, and, as with ponies, if driven off, will return from long distances at certain seasons."

In the same issue, it was reported a local rancher, Montford Johnson, had lost a number of cattle recently--"stolen and driven north." He learned they had been driven towards Childers Ferry and crossed at Red Oak Ford, on the Arkansas.

The open ranges provided easy accumulation of livestock. The Territory was sparsely populated and one could move around undetected for days without seeing another human being. It was said that the range was full of unbranded horses and cattle, and were easy pickings by Posey, and his men who made regular forays into Texas and Southern Indian Territory gathering herds that were taken to Coffeyville and sold.

For some unknown reason Posey broke his rule of not bothering local livestock. He had been accused of cattle theft in the pages of the Indian Journal, but denied the charge, even sending in a compatriot to lodge complaint with the editor. But now the U.S. Marshal at Fort Smith had received a formal complaint by Charles Clinton, that Posey, and a man named Charles Cain, had stolen 40 head of his cattle, valued at four hundred dollars.

Clinton, a white man who was a resident of the Indian country, Western District of Arkansas, signed the complaint. Witnesses were listed as Clinton; Dan Childers, the Lighthorse captain; and Fred Severs, a highly respected Creek citizen living on the Arkansas River in the northern Creek country. Severs would later become secretary for the popular Creek Chief, Pleasant Porter, and would build the Severs Hotel in Muskogee, the largest hotel in the area at the time. Though the cattle theft was committed on the first of June 1876, the arrest order for Posey and Cain was not issued until April 5, 1877.

Coke and Hubbard appeared to be under pressure to bring Posey to justice in Texas. The executive order from Gov. Hubbard to Chief Coachman for Posey's arrest could not be ignored. Now came troubles with Judge Parker's federal court and with citizens in the territory in which he lived. The cattle stealing complaint lodged in Fort Smith was a federal law violation, even more serious than state laws.

With these new developments, the outlaw career of Bill Posey appeared to be nearing an end.

THE STATE OF TEXAS.

EXECUTIVE DEPARTMENT.

AUSTIN. *March 27* 1877

TO THE *Superintendent or Chief Executive Officer of the Indian Country*

Whereas, It appears by the annexed documents, which are hereby certified to be authentic, that *W. A. Posey*

stand s charged with *the crime of "Theft"*

committed in the State of Texas, and information having been received that the said *W. A. Posey* ha s fled from justice, and ha s taken refuge in *The Indian Territory*

Now, therefore, I, *R. B. Hubbard* Governor of the State of Texas, have thought proper, in pursuance of the provisions of the Constitution and Laws of the United States, to demand the surrender of the said *W. A. Posey* as fugitive from justice, and that *he be* delivered to *Daniel Childers* who *is* hereby appointed the Agent on the part of the State of Texas to receive *him*

GIVEN UNDER MY HAND, and the Great Seal of the State affixed, at the City of Austin, this the *27th* day of *March* A. D. One Thousand Eight Hundred and Seventy. *Seven*, and of the Independence of the United States the *One Hundred & first* and of Texas the *Forty Second* year.

Proclamation

By the Governor of the
State of Texas
$500 Reward
To all to whom these presents
shall come

Whereas it has been
made known to me that
On the 3rd day of May A.D.
1872 W. A. Posey was by the
judgment of the District Court
for McLennan County in
the State of Texas convicted
of felony and sentenced
to confinement in the State
penitentiary to hard Labor
for the period five years,
Whereas said W. A. Posey
after said Conviction
escaped from Custody and
is now at large and
a fugitive from justice
Now Therefore
I Richard Coke
Governor of the State of
Texas, by virtue of the
authority vested in
me by the Constitution
and laws of said State
do hereby offer a reward

of Five Hundred Dollars
for the arrest and delivery
of the said W. A. Posey
to the proper authorities
of the State penitentiary of
Texas inside of the
penitentiary gates

In Testimony whereof
I have hereunto signed
my name and caused
the Great seal of the
State to be affixed at
the City of Austin
this, the 4th day of
March A.D. 1874
(Signed)   Richard Coke
                    Governor
By the Governor,
A. W. DeBerry
          Secretary of State

— Copy —

BILL POSEY'S DRAMATIC END

As the time neared for Susan to give birth to Posey's fourth child, he moved the family to their second home near Concharte Town in the northern Creek country. It was a severe winter, and Susan could be near relatives who could help her with the new baby's delivery and aftercare. The new arrival was another son, whom they named Henry. The harsh winter finally loosened its icy grip, and the family began making preparations to relocate to their main home on Cane Creek, midway between Muskogee and Okmulgee.

Posey was making some repairs to the wagon that would move the family, and had it placed on wagon jacks. His two oldest sons, Matthew and Albert, were helping with the repairs, when suddenly the wagon slipped from a jack, trapping Posey's hand in between. The accident nearly severed his right index finger at the first joint. Susan wrapped the damaged hand and finger in a soft cloth and soaked it in kerosene to ward off infection. He would leave the next morning for Okmulgee, where he would have the wound attended by a doctor.

Arriving by horseback the next morning, Posey sought out a doctor in the tiny capital town of the Creek Nation. The mangled finger could not be saved, the doctor told him, and it would necessary to amputate the tip of the finger to the first joint, which he did. The doctor gave Posey a hard block of ivory to bite down on while the surgery and treatment were completed. There was no medication to ease the throbbing pain. With his hand swollen and heavily bandaged, Posey set out for the return journey home.

While in Okmulgee, Posey stopped to buy some groceries and other family supply needs. It did not take long for word to reach Chief Ward Coachman that Posey was in town. Coachman summoned a Creek Lighthorse Captain, Suntharlpee, with orders to capture Posey for the Texas authorities. The captain contacted two of his fellow officers, and they began to follow the trail of the fugitive. Posey had a good head start before Suntharlpee was able to get his chosen assistants and set out in pursuit.

The Lighthorsemen finally tracked Posey through a thickly wooded area of rolling hills, emerging in a brushy bottom where the Pole Cat Creek entered the Arkansas River. Posey was driving six head of stolen horses ahead of him. The area is near the present town of Jenks, just west of present Tulsa. Confronting Posey, Suntharlpee told the fugitive that Chief Coachman had ordered his arrest to be held for Texas authorities.

Posey, remembering the harsh and cruel conditions of the Texas penitentiary, vowed he would not be taken alive. He reached for his Henry repeating rifle, but was unable to get off one shot because of his swollen and bandaged hand. When Posey made the move for his gun, one of the Lighthorsemen leveled a double barrel shotgun down on him and pulled the trigger. The gun, a 10-gauge, loaded with .00 buckshot, exploded with a thunderous roar. The slugs struck Posey in the right arm, breaking it instantly.

With his right arm dangling uselessly by his side, Posey reached for a revolver with his left hand, getting off two errant shots before another charge of buckshot tore into his left shoulder, almost blowing it away. Both arms were now broken, and taken out of the fight. The outlaw then dug his spurs into the flanks of his horse, sending the animal into a full charge against the captain's mount. The impact caused Suntharlpee's horse to fall, dumping the captain into a nearby streambed.

Posey then spun his horse around upon the posse, who did not have time to reload the shotgun, but stood their ground, firing at him with revolvers. One slug tore off the end of Posey's nose, but still he kept coming and charging the officers with his horse. Other bullets from the revolvers found their mark, but the onslaught by Posey continued. He was riddled with bullets, and badly wounded, but seemed unstoppable. The Lighthorsemen feared he would again escape the clutches of the law.

All the bullets in the officers' revolvers had been spent before Suntharlpee was finally able to emerge from the creek bed, shaken and wet, to rejoin the fight. The captain, standing on the ground, pulled the trigger on his last shot at the charging horse and rider. The bullet struck Posey under the chin, breaking his jaw, and exploded through his brain. Mangled beyond belief, Posey then fell dead from his horse, at the feet of the Lighthorse Captain.

The body lay where it fell overnight. Friends and relatives came the next day to view the battle site and bury the body of the slain outlaw. Posey's remains were too mangled to even be washed by water from the nearby creek. A coffin was hastily nailed together from wooden planks that had been brought in.

Posey was wrapped in a hand made blanket sent him by his mother when his sons had come to live with him in the Territory. His body was placed into the coffin, and buried near a large boulder, where he had fallen during the battle. There was no minister to deliver last words, or a prayer for comfort in the afterlife.

The killing of Posey by the Lighthorse commanded attention far and wide. Newspaper accounts of the events were wired across the United States and several foreign countries. Many visitors came to view the site where the battle occurred and to see the freshly dug grave in the creek bottom.

Following Posey's death, Susan took the infant, Henry, and went to live with a family named Grayson near Uchee Town. The three Posey sons by Elizabeth; Matthew, Albert and Robert, were taken in by Posey's cousin, Lucinda Ann (Hopwood) Smith. Lucinda was a one-quarter Creek through the Berryhill bloodline, and lived in the Concharte area, near the place where Posey had been killed.

The U.S. Indian Agent, S.W. Marston, sent a communiqué from his Muskogee office to Chief Coachman regarding Posey's fate. The message, dated June 20, 1877, was short and simple. It read:

"Sir: I have learned through what I believe to be a reliable source that the Light Horsemen of Muskokee (sic) District in attempting the arrest of Wm. A. Posey who was demanded some time ago by the Governor of the State of Texas was forced to kill him. You will please report all the facts in this case to this office at as early a day as they can be obtained from your officers."

Another letter from Marston to the Chief, dated July 2, 1877, contained this message:

"Dear Sir: I have received from his Excellency the Governor of Texas in regard to the killing of William A. Posey in an attempt to secure his capture upon the Governor's requisition & all is satisfactory. I have therefore concluded it would be best for you to retain the Governor's requisition papers in the files of your office & so I return it to you for this purpose."

A white man named Henry Riggs, claiming he was Posey's brother-in-law, charged Suntharlpee and his men had kept Posey's weapons, and he wanted them turned over to him. This affair caught the attention of Jacob Barnett, a Judge of the Deep Fork District of the Creek Nation, who wrote a letter to Chief Coachman, dated June 22, 1877:

"Dear Sir: This man Riggs, a white man living near Col. Robinson's in the Deep Fork District, and a brother-in-law to Bill Posey is meddling himself I think too much for a man in his position and status in this country. I have learned that he has written a letter to some of the U.S. Marshals concerning the killing of Posey and also about Captain Suntharlpee taking Posey's arms. I have no idea that he can do anything but it goes to show that he wants to meddle where he has no business--and cause trouble so I must advise you to revoke his permit immediately and report him as an intruder and let the Nation get rid of him for I think he is a bad man."

It is believed Riggs was a brother of Posey's second wife, Susan. His name was Henry Riggs, and the new Posey son had been named Henry. All Posey's sisters had married except Piety Jane Posey, who still resided with her parents in Limestone County. She never married. None of Posey's sisters were married to a man by the name of Riggs.

A letter signed by Judge Micco of the Deep Fork District, dated September 25, 1877, told Chief Coachman that the prosecuting attorney for the district had informed him that Henry Riggs was, indeed, an intruder in the Muskokee (sic) Nation and his permit to reside in the Territory had expired some time before.

Thus ended the life of William Andrew Jackson Posey, in a violent and bloody shoot-out in the wilderness of Indian Territory. He had spent the last five of his 31years as a fugitive from the law. He had lost his land, his wife, his herds of livestock, and his dreams with them. At the end he did have his sons, perhaps his most prized possession.

Strangely, it was never known what caused the rift between Bill Posey and his brother-in-law, Matt Wallace. The two men were very close at one time. They were the same age, were childhood friends, had served in the confederate army together, and Posey had married Wallace's sister. His first-born son was named Matthew Andrew, a combination of their two names. They even lived as neighbors.

There is no question about a falling out between the two men. Could it have been the loss of land inherited by Sarah Ann Miller-Wallace they would never be paid for? Posey had signed a promissory note, but a deed had been executed that conveyed ownership to Posey. The land was then lost to satisfy judgment in civil lawsuits. Posey was very upset at the loss of property and his sentence to the penitentiary. He went to the homes of the lawyers and the doctor threatening their lives.

Was there a bloodletting oath among family members to never discuss the events? Even first generation descendants were not even aware that Posey was implicated in the lynching of Matt Wallace.

Posey descendants say, according to family legend, Matt Wallace had stolen a horse and the sheriff was close behind. Wallace supposedly came to the home of Posey where he corralled the animal, which had been ridden hard and was all lathered up. The Posey family was not at home, so he selected a fresh horse from Posey's corral, leaving the telltale stolen horse behind. The sheriff, finding the stolen animal, arrested Posey, charging him with theft of the animal.

McLennan County Court records do not reveal any single charges of horse theft against Posey. He faced some fifteen charges, but all were multiple thefts. Additionally, Matt Wallace was no more than a mile from home when he would have come to Posey's house since the Wallace and Posey families all lived on the Garza survey land.

Wallace descendants were told that Matt Wallace was out looking for strays and came upon rustlers stealing his animals, whereupon he was lynched by the thieves to avoid testimony and identification by him. It was also said the lynching occurred to keep Wallace from testifying against Posey on some theft charges. Matt Wallace, however, was not listed as a witness on any of the charges against Posey in the McLennan County Court records. Posey was faced with so many charges against him, with so many different witnesses that another charge and witness would have made little difference.

Washington Wallace, Matt Wallace, William Wallace and Robert Wallace were all charged initially with Bill Posey in the theft of livestock, altering cattle brands, violation of the estray law, etc. Charges then began to be filed against Posey individually. Court action was eventually dropped against all the Wallace men, and they were never in trouble with the law again.

The events of the forced removal of the eastern Indian tribes, the battle for Texas Independence, the Civil War, and the Reconstruction period were some of the most turbulent times in U.S. and Texas history. The fate of the people living during this period shows a strength and determination for survival, yet a confidence in the future. They accepted the challenges of this unsettled existence on a day-to-day basis. Above all, they were a brave people.

For whatever path they trod, be it saint or sinner, the families of Miller, Lott, Lynch, Cohron, Aikman, Wallace, Posey and Lehmann were a part of this history. Their blood was shed on the Texas Bluebonnets. May they rest in peace.

Tough People for tough Texas times

All were cowboys on the Chisholm Trail

Bill Posey, 1846-1877
Became outlaw and was
killed in a bloody shoot-out in
Indian Territory

Max Lehmann, 1854-1904
Came to Texas as an infant from
Germany. Became a cowboy,
raised family of eight. Murdered
in 1904 near Carrizo Springs, TX.

The Wallace Family Saw Terror On The Tehuacana

When the Posey gang murdered Matthew Wallace their lives were changed forever. They left the Waco area never to return. Posey became an outlaw in Indian Territory.

W. S. Wallace
1824-1914
ca. 1910

W.W. Wallace
1850-1933
ca. 1924

R. W. Wallace
1853-1930
ca. 1920

The Aftermath

Following the death of Bill Posey, Susan and the infant Henry Posey went to live with her family near Concharty and Red Fork. The three other Posey sons were taken in by their Berryhill-Hopwood kin, but were soon kicked out because of Matthew. Matthew was troublesome and difficult to control. They drifted to Utah and Idaho where they worked as cowboys. They returned to Indian Territory periodically to visit family. Matthew lost an arm at the shoulder in a bank robbery shootout, reportedly as a member of the Dalton gang. Matthew's daughter said he never talked about his past or the loss of the arm. He could roll a Bull Durham cigarette with one hand, she said. [45]

Bill Posey's sons were each one-quarter Creek. Each was awarded a 160-acre allotment of land by the Dawes Commission. The land was soon sold, however, and they continued to live in Indian Territory and Utah.

Dan Childers

The former Creek Lighthorseman went berserk in the summer of 1885. He first went down to Muskogee where he had a tombstone made for himself with only the date blank. He then drove his light wagon up the trail to Tulsa, lashing his team and raving incoherently. He then stopped at a store and bought three coffins, drove out to Red Fork and killed his sister-in-law. He loaded the body into the wagon and returned to Tulsa, raging and terrorizing the town. Childers headed out to the ranch of George Perryman, bent on more murder. He was shot dead as he approached the house. Perryman, a kindly Creek Indian, took the dead man's children into his family and reared and educated them as his own.

Captain Suntharlpee

Suntharlpee, the Creek Lighthorse Captain who delivered the fatal shot to Bill Posey, became prominent in Creek politics. He built a house and a blacksmith shop near Euchee Town and served as a member of the U.S. Indian police in the Tulsa area. He also served as a cattle inspector at Red Fork, I.T.

Charles Clinton

Clinton was the white rancher who claimed Bill Posey and Charles Cain had stolen 40 head of cattle from his range. He was intermarried with a Creek woman and formerly lived in Okmulgee. He built a 10-room home on a hilltop out of Tulsa and moved his family there. His wife was a former student at the Tullahassee Indian School. She was a teacher in the neighboring schools. Clinton built a ferry across the Arkansas River near Red Fork, which was a big shipping center for cattle in later years.

William Crabtree

William Crabtree was a Limestone County punk who had come to Texas from Arkansas in the late 1860s. He was in and out of jail accused of many crimes and was a known member of the Posey gang. He was implicated in the lynching of Matt Wallace and jailed at Waco, but the charges were dismissed for lack of evidence. The 1878 murder of J.T. Vaughn, a citizen of Bosque County, Texas implicated Crabtree. The Horrell brothers out of Lampasas had been charged with the murder with the trial being held in Meridian, county seat of Bosque County. Crabtree had turned state's evidence during that trial in testimony about the brutal robbery and murder of Vaughn resulting in the conviction of the Horrell brothers. Crabtree was shot to death on November 28. His body, bearing six bullet holes to the chest, was found in a ravine near the Meridian courthouse. Lawmen attributed the killing of Crabtree to friends of the Horrell brothers, revenge for his testimony against the men. [50]

Last Posey Member Caught

A Waco, Texas dispatch October 21, 1887 said: "Twelve or fifteen years since there was a desperate gang of horse and cattle thieves located in the jungles of Tehuacana, about ten miles from Waco, under the lead of the celebrated desperado Bill Posey. The band had consisted of Posey, Bud and Ben Fuller, William Crabtree, the Sweats and others. Posey was since killed. Crabtree was killed. Sweat served a five years sentence, and yesterday morning Deputy Marshal Waller arrested Ben Fuller near Caddo, in the Indian Territory, and landed him in the Waco jail.

Fuller had been a fugitive from justice for seven years and only lived with his Winchester constantly in his hand. Waller only succeeded in arresting him by some neat strategy for which he is noted. Fuller has been indicted for horse and cattle thefts in many cases."

Thus fell the last member of one of the most desperate bands of lawless outlaws and ruffians with which the frontiers of Texas and Indian Territory had been infested.

AN EPILOG OF THE TEHUACANA FAMILIES:

Following the tragic events of Matt Wallace's death and the loss of lands, the Wallace family left the Tehuacana, relocating to Llano County. Louisa and Sarah Ann, now widows, took their children and relocated to Marble Falls, in Burnet County. From there the lives of all would take on new perspectives.

Louisa Lott

Louisa had witnessed Texas history from its beginning as a possession of Spain and Mexico in Austin's colony, through the Republic of Texas period, and into statehood. Hers had not been an easy life. She had been widowed three times, and had children by all three husbands. Louisa's daughters had married and left home, although they remained in a close geographic proximity. It is said she married a fourth time to a man named Breslin. No children were born to this marriage. Louisa's two sons by Aikman became farmers. They lived in Burnet, Caldwell, Travis and Milam counties.

Family lore tells Pitts Aikman and his stepfather had an argument one day in the field. Breslin proceeded to give the youth a thrashing. Pitts came back to the house to retrieve a gun to continue the episode. Louisa, it was said, took the gun away from Pitts and ordered Breslin to leave. As Pitts and Will matured, they each married girls from the Prairie Lea community in Caldwell County, later moving to Milam County where they farmed for many years.

Louisa's children by Robert T. Miller:

*CELIA (CECELIA) FRANCES MILLER, was born in 1850 on the Tehuacana Creek homestead near Waco. She married Benjamin Bruce Lofland of Limestone County, September 26, 1867, at Waco. They lived at Springfield, but later moved to Wise County, where Lofland was engaged in farming and stock raising.

They had one daughter, "Pinkie," born in September 1888. Celia and Ben Lofland were divorced in 1897. Celia died in 1900. Pinkie married David Floyd Cude in 1904. They had three children: Otis Rayford, 1905; Vera Mae, 1907 and Pinkie Evelyn, 1912. They moved to Salt Lake City, Utah in 1924.

*SARAH ANN MILLER was born March 22, 1852, on the Tehuacana Creek homestead. She married Matthew Alexander Wallace. They had two children, Sarah Emmaline Wallace and Matthew Alexander Wallace, II. Sarah's husband, Matt Wallace, was lynched in their own front yard in events previously reported. She married Max Lehmann in 1877. The report will continue under the Max Lehmann family.

Louisa's children by Hamilton C. Cohron:

*ELIZABETH COHRON was born in 1855. Little is known about Elizabeth. She is shown in the 1860 Limestone County census with the Cohron family. She is shown again in the 1870 McLennan County census with the Albert Aikman family, age 15. It is believed she died sometime after that census. Deeds of record from Louisa, Laura Jane and Ellen, the heirs of the H.C. Cohron estate, indicate the three had full ownership. Had Elizabeth still been living, a deed would have been necessary from her since she would have shared in the estate by law.

*LAURA JANE COHRON, was born September 25, 1858, in Limestone County. She married Robert Wiley Wallace. Their profile will be continued with the Wallace family epilog.

*ELLEN R. COHRON, was born July 29, 1861, in Limestone County. She married William W. Wallace. A profile on each will be continued with the Wallace family epilog.

Louisa's children by Albert A. Aikman:

*PITTS AIKMAN was born December 13, 1868, in McLennan County. He married Mattie Viola Barnes at Prairie Lea, Texas, July 12, 1894. They were parents of seven children; Cora Icy, born in

1895 in Travis County; William Wesley, born in 1896 in Falls County, who died in infancy; Luther Roscoe, born in 1897 in Falls County. The others, all born in Milam County, include Esther Josephine, born in 1901; Robert Newton, born in 1905, who died in infancy; and twins, Oscar Jennings, and Katie Lee, born in 1907. Pitts Aikman died July 13, 1936. He was 68 years of age. Mattie Viola died April 23, 1950. They are both buried in South Elm Cemetery, northwest of Cameron, Texas.

*WILLIAM SMITH AIKMAN was born February 11, 1872, in McLennan County. He and Camilla Rusha Polk, of Prairie Lea, were married June 10, 1893, at Prairie Lea. They were parents of six children; Archie Dexter, 1895; Viola Lovie, 1896; Minnie Lee, 1901; Ophelia, 1905; Melvin Ivy; 1910, and Pearlie Sue, born in 1913. Viola was born blind, but was able to do many things, including playing the game of "hide-and-seek" with her playmates. The family lived for many years in Milam and Falls counties, but later moved to Hico, Texas. Will died May 25, 1948, at age 76. Camilla died January 3, 1967. They are both buried in Powers Chapel Cemetery, Rosebud, Texas.

Louisa spent her later years sharing time with the families of her son, and daughter, Pitts Aikman and Laura Jane Wallace. She died in 1911, while living with Robert and Laura Jane Wallace, at Axtell, Texas. She was 83 years of age. She is buried in Axtell Cemetery, within a few miles of the spot on Tehuacana Creek where she first settled in 1846 with Robert T. Miller.

Louisa Lott was a true Texas pioneer.

MARY CECELIA MILLER / JOSEPH P. LYNCH FAMILY

Mary Cecelia Miller was born March 19, 1820, in Rapides Parish, Louisiana, the daughter of Andrew Miller and Celia Neal. She died June 12, 1852, at age 32.

Joseph Penn Lynch was born in Kentucky in 1810. His parentage is not known. He died in 1861. Both are buried in the old Springfield Cemetery, now Fort Parker State Park, near Groesbeck,

Texas. Both have markers.

Children of Mary Cecelia Miller and Jos. P. Lynch:

*WILLIAM ANDREW LYNCH was born June 16, 1838, at Washington-on-the-Brazos. He served in the Terry's Texas Ranger unit during the Civil War and was wounded twice in the same day in battles at Rome, Ga. He was a resident of Limestone County. He never married. Despondent over the war injuries that never healed, he committed suicide in 1869. His place of burial is unknown.

*JOSEPH MILAM LYNCH was born June 24, 1840, at Washington-on-the-Brazos. He was a farmer and stock raiser. Lynch's first wife, Mary Roxanna Wallace, died in childbirth. Their only child, William Andrew Lynch, was raised by his Wallace grandparents. The second wife of J.M. Lynch was Mary Ellen Hunt, of Kaufman County. They were parents of four children, including another son named William Joseph. Lynch farmed in northeastern Kaufman County. He died May 6, 1891, and is buried at College Mound Cemetery in Kaufman County.

*ANNIE ELIZA LYNCH was born March 1, 1841, at Washington-on-the-Brazos. She married William Calvit. She died March 11, 1928, and is buried in Wareville Cemetery, Utopia, Texas.

*MARY ETTA LYNCH was born July 5, 1845, at Washington-on-the-Brazos. She married Capt. William B. Waldrom, March 6, 1866. One child, Annie Katie Waldrom, was born February 7, 1870. Mary Etta died May 16, 1874, age twenty nine, at their home near Butler, Freestone County, Texas. Following the death of Mary Etta, Waldrom married her sister, Lucretia P. Lynch, who was already living in the household. Lucretia (Lula) raised their daughter. Waldrom and Lucretia had no children born to them. Lucretia died August 7, 1889, at age thirty eight. Waldrom died in August, 1933, at age ninety eight. The three are buried in Mayes Cemetery, near the Lone Star community, southwest of Palestine. Waldrom's parents, and a sister, are also buried in the Waldrom family plot.

*LAURA CECELIA LYNCH was born May 15, 1847, at Washington-on-the-Brazos. She married Neal Davidson at Alexandria, La., in September 1868. They moved to Limestone County in 1872. Davidson bought all the William Andrew Lynch estate properties in several counties for one dollar per acre in the estate sale. Laura's uncle, Merideth Neal Miller, was administrator of the estate. Davidson died September 18, 1878, at age thirty four in a yellow fever epidemic. He is buried at Honest Ridge Cemetery in Limestone County. The widow, Laura Cecelia Davidson, was left with two children; Lynch Davidson, four, and Annie Laurie Davidson, age one. Lynch Davidson apprenticed in the lumber business, then opened his own lumber company in Laredo and Houston, and became a multi-millionaire. Davidson operated the Southland lumber yards in Oklahoma and Texas. He served in the Texas House of Representatives, 1920-22, and as Lieutenant Governor of Texas from 1922-24. He was an unsuccessful candidate for Governor of Texas, being defeated in the Democrat primary by Miriam "Ma" Ferguson, who then became Texas' first woman governor. Laura died January 24, 1923, at the home of her son in Houston. She was seventy six. She is buried in Hollywood Cemetery, Houston, Texas.

*NATHANIEL H. LYNCH, was born January 26, 1849, at Springfield, in Limestone County. He died in infancy October 3, 1849. He is buried in old Springfield cemetery next to his parents. His grave is the oldest recorded grave there.

*LUCRETIA P. LYNCH was born January 24, 1851, at Springfield, Limestone County. She died August 7, 1889, and is buried in Mayes Cemetery, at Lone Star community. (See above history with Mary Etta lynch and Capt. W.B. Waldrom).

THE MERIDETH NEAL MILLER/
LUCY ELLER OLIVER FAMILY

Merideth Neal Miller was born November 20, 1828, in Washington County, Texas. His father, Andrew Miller, died in 1838, when Merideth was only ten years of age. His mother married John Lott, and they moved to Grimes County. Merideth was sent to live with Neal relatives in Louisiana, where he attended school. He returned to Texas, settling in Limestone County. In 1850, he bought land at Horn Hill, where he ranched. Sometime later he bought land at Honest Ridge, where he lived for thirty years. He married Lucy Eller Oliver, March 14, 1854. They were parents of eight children. Merideth was a successful rancher and businessman. At the time of his death he owned 1,000 acres of land, and a cotton gin. He died September 17, 1884, at age fifty six. He is buried in Honest Ridge Cemetery. Lucy died December 8, 1897. It is presumed she is buried beside Merideth, although his is the only marker in the family burial plot. Two infant sons are also buried beside Merideth.

The Children of Merideth Neal Miller and Lucy Eller Oliver:

*ANDREW NEAL MILLER was born January 11, 1855, in Limestone County. He was married to Mattie Greer Lane, and they had one child, Lillian Alline. Andrew was a rancher in Leon County. He died June 10, 1931, and is buried in Oakwood, Texas, cemetery.

*MARY ELLER MILLER was born in 1860, in Limestone County. She married John Thomas Davidson in 1879. They lived at Laredo, Texas, where Davidson was associated with Lynch Davidson in the lumber business. The dates of death, and place of burial for them is not known.

*ALLINE MILLER was born in March, 1863, in Limestone County. She married W.H. LeFevre, a minister, in 1884. They lived in several cities in Texas before settling in Hillsboro. Alline was owner and operator of an insurance agency for many years following the death of her husband. The dates of death for them is not known. They are buried in Hillboro Cemetery.

*LUCRETIA MILLER was born October 12, 1865, in Limestone County. She married James Rayford Wimbish, April 7, 1890. They lived in Limestone County, where he was a rancher. Lucretia died December 28, 1936. Both are buried in Faulkenberry Cemetery, Groesbeck, Texas.

*WILLIAM OLIVER MILLER was born in Limestone County, February 2, 1869. He was a rancher. He was married to Willie H. Mayes, April 23, 1894. He died May 23, 1937. She died August 7, 1963. Their Burial place is not known.

*ROSENA MILLER was born in 1871, in Limestone County. She married H.W. Williams, November 15, 1894. Death dates and burial place for either is not known.

*ORA MILLER was born in February, 1875, in Limestone County. She never married, and lived most of her life with her sister, Alline. Her death date is not known. She is buried in Hillsboro Cemetery.

*SAM HOUSTON MILLER was born in 1882, in Limestone County. He was a stockman. He never married, and lived with his brother, Andrew Neal Miller, and his sister, Alline Miller LeFevre, most of his life. His death date is unknown. He is buried in Hillsboro Cemetery.

LUCRETIA MILLER/FRANKLIN C. OLIVER FAMILY

Lucretia Miller was born in Washington County, Texas, in 1833, the daughter of Andrew and Celia Neal Miller. She was only five years of age when her father was killed. Celia Miller then married John Lott, and the family moved across the Brazos River to Grimes County, where Lott had a plantation. After Jos. P. and Mary Miller Lynch moved from Washington to Springfield, Lucretia lived with their family until she met and married Franklin C. Oliver in September, 1850. Frank Oliver was a stockraiser and merchant at Fairfield, in Freestone County. He continued in business until the outbreak of the Civil War. In 1866, the family moved to Limestone County, where he continued in stockraising and farming. In 1885, he and his son, John E. Oliver, formed a mercantile partnership as F.C. Oliver & Son, in Groesbeck. The firm handled furniture, hardware and farm implements. Frank Oliver died May 12, 1902, at age seventy five. Lucretia died October 3, 1903, at age seventy. Both are buried in Faulkenberry Cemetery, Grosebeck, Texas.

Children of Lucretia Miller and Frank C. Oliver:

*THOMAS W. OLIVER was born in 1852, in Freestone County. He married Alice Traweek, of Limestone County, in 1870. He died in 1884. His place of burial is not known.

*JOHN E. OLIVER was born in Freestone County, August 28, 1854. He married Pauline Bennett, in 1874. He was a successful farmer, stockman and merchant in Groesbeck. The dates of death and place of burial for John and Pauline Oliver is not known.

*O.D. OLIVER was born in 1858, in Freestone County. He married Carrie Lanier Burney, September 20, 1882. She was the daughter of attorney and district judge, James I. Burney. O.D. was called "Dee," or "D." He was a banker and stockraiser in Groesbeck. He died in 1932. Carrie died in 1938. Both are buried in Faulkenberry Cemetery, Groesbeck.

*WALTER S. OLIVER was born in 1859, in Freestone County. He was a stock trader and real estate dealer in the Dallas area. He later moved to the Edmond, Oklahoma area. His family history, date of death and place of burial is not known.

*MARY (Mollie) OLIVER was born November 12, 1868, in Limestone County. She married Rev. Edward Tate Harrison. They were parents of three children. She died July 16, 1949. Her place of burial is unknown.

The Children of Sarah Ann Miller

Sarah's children with Matthew A. Wallace

Sarah EmmalineWallace
1871-1938

Sarah Emmmaline Wallace-Faught was two years of age and witnessed the lynching of her father in Waco, Texas in 1873.

Matthew A. Wallace II
1873-1952

Sarah was pregnant with Matthew Aexander Wallace II when his father was murdered by the Bill Posey gang.

Following the murder of Matthew Wallace by the Bill Posey gang, Sarah and Max Lehmann were married

Sarah Miller Wallace-Lehmann
1852-1900

Max Lehmann, 1854-1904
Was murdered in 1904

Celia Frances Lehmann-Dunham
1878-1953

Louisa Lehmann-Halliburton,
1880-1973

The Lehmann Brothers, 1914
Jesse, Will, Max and Paul

The Lehmann brothers gathered at Lampasas, Texas in 1914 for the wedding of Will Lehmann to Mattie Warren. It would be the last time they were all together at the same time. The brothers:
Will Lehmann, 1882-1934
Jesse Lehmann, 1885-1970
Max Lehmann, 1890-1979
Paul Lehmann, 1892-?
Two Lehmann children failed to survive infancy. They were Henry Lehmann, 1884 and Wilhelmina Fredericka, 1888.

THE MAX LEHMANN/SARAH ANN MILLER FAMILY

Johann Maximilian (Max) Lehmann was born March 9, 1854, in Berlin, Germany. He immigrated with his father, Carl Ludwig Gustav, and brother Paul, to Indianola, Texas, in 1854. Paul was born in Berlin, Germany in 1852. The mother of Paul and Max was Adelphine Louisa Sperlinng, but she either died in Germany or on board the ship to America. Gustav, a widower, married Wilhelmina (mnu) in 1856 after arriving in Texas.

Gustav was born March 14, 1825, at Landsberg an der Warthe, Prussia. Wilhelmina was born September 25, 1824, in Hamburg, Germany. Gustav was employed with the Morgan Steamship lines. Indianola was a major port of entry to Texas, and large amounts of freight and passengers came into Indianola, where Gustav maintained a large wharf and warehouse for the steamship line. A daughter, Augusta, was born in 1862.

Gustav served three years and eight months with Company B, Eighth Texas Infantry, the Confederate Army, during the Civil War. He was taken prisoner when the Yankees sacked Indianola, and was a prisoner of war at camps in New Orleans and Shreveport, Louisiana until the end of the Civil War. Following discharge he resumed his duties with the steamship lines.

The Lehmann sons were apprentice butchers during their teen years. Max did not accept the stiff German discipline ethic, wanting to travel and find new experiences. In 1870, While barely 16, he left home and became a cowboy, gathering cattle and horses, and moving them north on the Chisholm Trail. He had become acquainted with an old Texas ranching family, the Halliburtons, of Gonzales County for whom he worked. Longhorn cattle were in great abundance in the mesquite thickets of south central Texas.

The movement of the Halliburton cattle through Waco caused the young Max to come in contact with the Posey and Wallace families. There he met Sarah Ann (Miller) Wallace. Following the death of Sarah's husband, Matthew Wallace, Max returned to court Sarah, and they were married in 1876.

Indianola was completely destroyed by a hurricane that came streaming in out of the Gulf of Mexico on September 15, 1875. Houses were swept away and businesses destroyed as the gulf waters and wind took their toll. The loss of life was estimated at 300, but the Lehmanns survived. The town quickly rebuilt, and it once again became an important seaport.

Disaster struck again when Indianola was swept away by another hurricane on August 19, 1886. This time the winds and rushing waters were much stronger. More than 500 residents were estimated to have lost their lives in this storm. Miraculously, the Lehmann family survived again.

Indianola was not rebuilt following the 1886 storm. Gustav, Wilhelmina and Paul moved inland to Cuero. Paul, the stable son, owned and operated a butcher shop in Cuero from 1887 until his death in 1907. Gustav died May 17, 1892, at age 68. Wilhelmina died January 19, 1901, at age 77. Paul died in March, 1907, at age 54. All are buried in the family burial plot in Hillside Cemetery, Cuero, Texas.

Max and Sarah lived for a time in Dallas County, where he farmed. The family is enumerated under the name of "John Lehman" in the 1880 Texas census for Dallas County. The two Wallace children are shown with the family, but are not separately identified. Celia Frances and Louisa Augusta, the first two Lehmann children, were probably born in Dallas County. They later lived at Marble Falls, Cuero, Gonzales and Luling, Texas where Max was a rural mail carrier and farmer. He loved racehorses, and always had some blooded racers in his stable.

The Lehmann family was living in Gonzales County when Sarah became ill with appendicitis. She died July 27, 1900, at age 48, and is buried in Belmont Cemetery, Gonzales County. Max then moved the family to Stockdale in Wilson County, where he was a rural mail carrier between Floresville and Stockdale. Max Lehmann was a murder victim when John Tumlinson shot him to death July 13, 1904 near Carrizo Springs, Texas. He had gone there to fetch the daughter of Tumlinson who had planned to marry Max.

Tumlinson objected to the marriage and killed Lehmann. Tumlinson fled to Mexico but was apprehended and spent a year in jail at Laredo, Texas. He was freed because of lack of evidence, he being the only witness to the killing. The burial place of Max Lehmann is inknown.

Following the death of Sarah and Max, their daughter, Louisa Augusta Lehmann-Halliburton, took the youngest children in her home. She had married Tack Halliburton in 1901, the son of Max's old rancher friend. They lived in Gonzales County, where Tack was a rancher.

Children of Sarah Ann Miller/Matthew A. Wallace:

*SARAH EMMALINE WALLACE was born September 7, 1871, at Waco, Texas. She married John William Faught and located to Dallas County. Seven children were born to the marriage: Sarah Elizabeth; Carrie; Lillie; David; Jerry; Clinton and Paul. She died March 18, 1938, at age sixty seven. J.W. Faught died April 7, 1941. They are both buried at Restland Memorial Park, Dallas, Texas.

*MATTHEW ALEXANDER WALLACE, II, was born August 26, 1873, at Waco, Texas. His father was murdered three months before he was born. He was married to Dora Polina Eversole, at Gonzales, Texas, November 10, 1896. Two sons were born to the marriage: Cecil, birthdate unknown, and Frank Alexander, October 16, 1897. His wife left the family, ca. 1900, going to Beaumont. Matt and the boys lived near Belton, in Bell County. Sarah was visiting with Matt and helping care for the boys when she was stricken with appendicitis and died.

Matt then married Alice Edith Herbert Youmans, in Bell County, in 1913. She had two children by a previous marriage: Herbert P. Youmans, born August 1, 1906, and Estherlene Youmans, born April 13, 1910.

Four children were born to the new marriage: Burl Richard, born August 27, 1914; Beulah Maureen, born April 18, 1916; Joseph Matthew, born December 8, 1917, and Billie Louise, born

February 7, 1920.

Tragedy struck the family when Alice died on December 19, 1923, just one week before Christmas. The older children by the former marriages had grown up and left home, but Matt was left with four very young children to raise.

Bad luck was to haunt the family again when fire destroyed their home July 4, 1924. Matt had taken the children into Belton to see the annual fireworks display. While they were away the house burned to the ground, taking everything except the clothes they were wearing. The family lived in a tent near the burned out house until the crops could be gathered and sold. They then moved to Dallas, where Matt was employed as a nurseryman.

Alice Edith Wallace is buried at Rest Haven Cemetery, near Belton. Matt Wallace, II, died June 8, 1952, at age seventy nine. He is buried at Restland Memorial Park Cemetery, Dallas, Texas.

Children of Max Lehmann/Sarah Ann Miller-Wallace:

*CELIA FRANCES LEHMANN, was born February 10, 1878. She was named for Sarah's sister. She married Newton Dunham in Gonzales County, August 24, 1896. They lived at Waelder, Texas, where Newt was employed with Gonzales County. Newton Dunham died in 1936, and is buried in Waelder Cemetery. Celia Frances later married Henry Owens and lived in Houston. She died December 23, 1953, and was buried on Christmas day in the Thompsonville, cemetery, near Waelder. Celia Frances and Newt Dunham reportedly had an adopted daughter, Irene. No further information is known.

*LOUISA AUGUSTA LEHMANN, was born September 17, 1880. She was named for Sarah's mother, Louisa Lott, and Max Lehmann's sister, Augusta Lehmann. She married Barthlomew T. "Tack" Halliburton, at Stockdale, Wilson County, in July, 1901. After the death of their Lehmann parents, Louisa took the three youngest boys, Jesse, Max and Paul, into the Halliburton home until they were old enough to leave. Six children were born to the Halliburtons: Max Meldrum, August 23, 1902; Robert Brooks,

1913; twin girls, Jessie and Bessie; Elma, and Gladys. Tack Halliburton died in March, 1946. Louisa died April 1, 1973. They are both buried in Waelder, Texas cemetery.

*WILLIAM CHARLES LEHMANN was born October 29, 1882, at Cuero, Texas. He married Martha (Mattie) Warren, August 19, 1914, at Lampasas, Texas. In 1918, they moved to Chouteau, Oklahoma, where he farmed and raised livestock. They moved to Muskogee in 1930, where he was a dairy superintendent. Three children were born to them: Dorothy Lee, 1916; John Ellis, 1920, who died in infancy; and William Eugene, 1928. Will Lehmann died March 16, 1934, at age 52. He is buried in Chouteau Cemetery. Mattie Lehmann died February 10, 1979, at age 79. She is also buried in Chouteau Cemetery. Will Lehmann was the father of this writer.

*HENRY LEHMANN was born October 28, 1884. He died in infancy. Place of burial is unknown.

*JESSE GASTER LEHMANN was born April 11, 1885. He married Adaline Lynn. They lived for a time at Lampasas and Florence, Texas, where Jesse farmed. They later moved to Austin, where he was employed at the University of Texas. Adaline was was first married to G.W. Lewis, and had one child, Zepha Estelle Lewis, born June 7, 1905. Jess and Addie were married September 8, 1907. They were parents of four children: Lynn Paul, born June 7, 1911; Lorena Catherine, born July 8, 1914; Willie Aline, born October 1, 1916, and Nancy Maxene, born June 19, 1919. Adeline died July 12, 1964. Jesse died December 19, 1970. Both are buried at Austin.

*WILHELMINA FREDERICA LEHMANN was born September 10, 1888. She died August 27, 1889, in infancy. Her place of burial is unknown.

*MAX MILBURN LEHMANN was born July 5, 1890, at Cuero, Texas. He was a veteran of WWI, enlisting in the U.S. Army in 1917. He was in the engineering corps as a bridge builder. He served a tour of duty in France, and was in the army of occupation of Germany. He was discharged in 1919. He married

Ruby Mayben, of Dallas, June 10, 1923. They lived in Garland most of their lives. They had one child, Max Milburn, Jr., who died in infancy. Max began a career as a truck driver with Craddock Foods Company, a large pickle processing plant. He then served as plant manager for many years. He loved fishing and horse racing. He retired in 1970. Max died January 7, 1979. He and Ruby are buried in Garland Cemetery.

*PAUL LEHMANN was born October 18, 1892. He was married to Ollie Lynn, June 26, 1916. Ollie was a sister to Adaline Lynn, who married Paul's brother, Jesse Lehmann. They lived at Lampasas. Paul disappeared two years after the marriage and was never heard from again.

THE WASHINGTON S. WALLACE FAMILY:

Washington S. Wallace and his family came to Texas from North Carolina sometime after 1850. They lived in Limestone County, near Springfield and Mt. Calm, later locating on the Lynch portion of the Garza survey, on Tehuacana Creek, in McLennan County. Wallace and his wife, Margaret, had six children, all of whom were born in North Carolina. Three of their sons married daughters of Louisa Lott. Following the family troubles, Wallace moved to Llano County. Margaret's death came sometime between 1870-80. Her death date and place of burial is unknown.

Wallace then married Mary Matilda (Reed) Burkett in Llano County, September 7, 1881. Mary Matilda had been widowed, with four children of her own: Ellen, Annie Laura, Virginia and Lavina. The family later moved to Fisher County, Texas, where Wallace was a farmer, and worked on the Texas & Pacific railroad. The family lived at Eskota, Texas. Wallace and Matilda had three children during their marriage, giving each second families. Wallace died November 11, 1914, at age ninety. He is buried at Palava, Texas. The death date of Mary Matilda Wallace is unknown. She is buried at Palava Cemetery, next to W.S. Wallace.

Children of Washington S. and Margaret Wallace:

*MATTHEW ALEXANDER WALLACE was born in 1846, in North Carolina. He married Sarah Ann Miller, a daughter of Louisa (Lott) Miller, in 1869. He died in June, 1873, a victim of a lynching. Matthew and Sarah were parents of two children: Sarah Emmaline, born in 1871, and Matthew Alexander, II, born in 1873. The place of burial is unknown for Matthew, Sr.

*MARY ROXANNA WALLACE was also born in 1846, according to census records. It is possible she and Matthew were twins. Mary Roxanna married Joseph Miller Lynch in 1867. One son, William Andrew Lynch, was born to them. Roxanna died either in childbirth or shortly thereafter. Her death date or place of burial is unknown. Her son, William Andrew Lynch, was raised by W.S. and Margaret Wallace. He married Annie Laura Burkett, a daughter of Mary Matilda, Wallace's second wife, ca. 1892. They had five children: Ruby, 1894; Finis W., 1896; Willie F., 1899; Lynn O., 1902, and Guy C. Lynch, 1905. Lynch and Annie Laura are both buried in Sweetwater Cemetery. William Andrew Lynch was employed with the Texas & Pacific railroad. While only an infant, in 1868, he was deeded the half interest of his father, Joseph Miller Lynch, in the Lynch property on Tehuacana Creek. He sold the land in 1893.

*ELIZABETH E. WALLACE, was born in 1848, in North Carolina. She married William Andrew Jackson Posey July 18, 1865. They had three sons: Matthew Andrew, born 1866; Albert Washington, born, 1869, and Robert A. Posey, born in 1871. All were born in McLennan County, near Waco. Elizabeth died in 1875, of what family members described as a broken heart. Her place of burial is near Waco in an unknown location. Following the death of Elizabeth, the sons were sent to live with their father in Indian Territory.

*SARAH C. WALLACE. Census records indicate he year of birth the same as Elizabeth, in 1848. It is possible there were two sets of twins in the family. This cannot be confirmed, however. Nothing more is known about Sarah Wallace. It is believed she died at an early age.

*WILLIAM W. WALLACE, was born in North Carolina, April 30, 1850. He married Ellen R. Cohron, a daughter of Louisa (Lott) Cohron, in 1876. They lived in McLennan, Young, Fort Bend, Bell and Bastrop Counties. Wallace was a farmer and stockraiser. In later years the couple managed a county nursing home facility in Bell County. They had fourteen children, of which eight lived. Ellen died September 13, 1926, and is buried in Elgin, Texas, cemetery. William W. Wallace died December 11, 1933. He is buried in Brown Cemetery, Okay community, near Killeen, Bell County, Texas.

The children of William and Ellen Wallace: George Washington, born 1876, in Llano County; Bettie R., born 1877, in Llano County; Matthew Alexander, born 1882; Dan C., born 1887; Eva B., born 1890; Clara Maud, born 1893, in Caldwell County; Jesse Vivian, born 1896, and Josephine, born in 1898.

*ROBERT WILEY WALLACE was born October 16, 1853, in North Carolina. He married Laura Jane Cohron, a daughter of Louisa (Lott) Cohron, in 1874. They went with the other Wallace family members to Llano County and Burnet Counties, but later returned to Limestone County where Robert farmed near the Ben Hur community. He retired, ca. 1905, buying a full block and a half of town lots in Axtell, Texas. Laura's mother, Louisa, lived with the family. Louisa died in 1911. Laura Jane died June 30, 1929. Robert died September 27, 1930. All are buried in the southeast quadrant of the Axtell cemetery. Robert and Laura Jane Wallace were parents of eleven children, of which eight lived. Three died in infancy: Laura, Andrew and Jesse. The living children were: John Wesley, born 1875; Maudie May, 1881; Robert Wiley, 1883, born in Burnet County; Ellen Marie, 1889; Arthur Daniel, 1890, born in Burnet County; Lillie L., 1891; Eunice Earle, 1893, and Lena Bessie, 1894.

The Children of Washington S. and Mary Matilda Wallace:

*WALTER EDGAR WALLACE was born in 1883, in Llano County, Texas. He married Alice I. Sherrod. They were parents of five children, and lived in Taylor County, near Abilene. He was a section foreman for the Texas & Pacific railroad. Their children were: Ruth, born 1905; Cecil, 1908; Lester, 1910; Loyd, 1914, and Mary, 1917. Walter and Alice are both buried in Elmwood Cemetery, Abilene, Texas.

*LILLIE PEARL WALLACE was born in Fisher County, Texas, in 1886. She married Brack Mitchell, of Nolan County. He was a farmer. They were parents of five children: Loy, born in 1904; Dick, born in 1906; Mary J., 1910; Minnie L., 1913, and Anna Belle, born in 1915. Lillie Pearl died March 31, 1944. The death date for Brack is not known. Both are buried in Sweetwater cemetery.

*ANNA BELLE WALLACE was born in August, 1889, in Fisher County. She married Michael M. Risinger, a physician, ca. 1905. They had four children: Michael O., born in 1906; Areta, born 1909; Maggie M., born in 1914, and Wallace Risinger, born ca. 1921. The family lived in Fisher County, but later moved to Grimes County briefly where Risinger practiced medicine at Anderson. They then moved to Roscoe.

Dr. Risinger was killed January 3, 1933, when a freight train struck his car at an intersection west of Roscoe. An influenza epidemic had kept him moving constantly in treating his patients. Family sources said he had not slept in more than twenty four hours preceding the accident. Dr. Risinger is buried in the I.O.O.F. cemetery at Roscoe. Anna Belle later married Jimmy Likes, and they lived in California. Likes preceded her in death. Anna Belle in later years lived with her son, Michael, in Hobbs, N.M. She died at age ninety two and is buried at Roscoe, Texas.

THE BENJAMIN FRANKLIN POSEY/
ELIZA BERRYHILL FAMILY

Benjamin Franklin Posey and Eliza Berryhill Posey were first cousins. They were married December 20, 1824, in Troup County, Georgia. They were each one-half Creek Indian. They were parents of fifteen children. They migrated to Texas in 1847, settling first at Nacogdoches, and then to Horn Hill, in Limestone County. Benajamin F. Posey was a rancher. Several of their children preceded the parents in death, and are buried in Horn Hill Cemetery, a plot of land donated by Posey, and at one time known as Posey Cemetery. Eliza Berryhill Posey died in 1881, at age seventy four. She is buried at Groesbeck, Texas. Benjamin F. Posey died in 1883, at age seventy seven, while visiting relatives in Indian Territory. His burial place is unknown.

*SARAH ANN POSEY was born in Troup County, Ga., in 1825. She married Silas H. Barber, in 1846. She died in 1868, and is believed buried in Hill County, Texas.

*THOMAS BERRYHILL POSEY was born September 9, 1826, in Troup County, Ga. He married Hulda Elizabeth Hughes in 1849. They both died in 1899, and are buried in Wagoner, I.T. Cemetery, (now Oklahoma). He was a rancher.

*PIETY JANE POSEY was born in 1828, in Chambers County, Ala. She never married. Piety Jane died February 9, 1887, and is buried in the Horn Hill Cemetery.

*BENJAMIN BELL POSEY was born in 1829, in Chambers County, Ala. He married Matilda Murphy in 1853. He died in 1864. His place of burial is unknown. He was a rancher.

*JOHN DEACH POSEY was born in 1831, in Chambers County, Ala. He married Catherine Jones in 1852. He died in 1896. His place of burial is unknown. He was a rancher.

*MARTHA ELMIRA POSEY was born in 1832 , in Chambers County, Ala. She married William Jacob Mayfield in 1859. She died in 1882. Her place of burial is unknown.

*NARCISSA POSEY was born in 1832, in Chambers County,

Alabama. She died in infancy.

*URIAH POSEY was born in Tallapoosa County, Ala., in 1836. He married Elizabeth Barlow in 1864. He died in 1877, and is buried in Horn Hill Cemetery. He was a rancher.

*NANCY GREEN POSEY was born in 1837, in Tallapoosa County, Ala. She married Chas. D. Oswalt in 1859. She died in 1867. Her burial place is in Horn Hill Cemetery.

*ELI POSEY was born in 1839, in Tallapoosa County, Ala. He married Mary Frances Neill in 1859. He died in 1875, and is buried in Horn Hill Cemetery. He was a rancher.

*TINSLEY ELIZABETH POSEY was born in 1841, in Tallapoosa County, Ala. She first married John Stinson in 1864. After his death, she married Silas H. Barber, the former husband of her sister, who had died. She died in 1874, and is buried in Horn Hill cemetery.

*JAMES MARION POSEY was born in 1842 in Tallapoosa County, Ala. He married Virginia A.C. Allen in 1866. He died in 1870. Both are buried in Horn Hill Cemetery. He was a rancher.

*GEORGE WASHINGTON POSEY was born in 1844, in Tallapoosa County, Ala. He never married. He died in 1863, of fever. He is buried in Limestone County.

*WILLIAM ANDREW JACKSON POSEY was born in Tallapoosa County, Ala., in 1846. He married Elizabeth Wallace in 1865, in Limestone County. They lived near Waco. Three sons were born to them: Matthew Andrew, Albert Washington and Robert A. Posey. Their profile will be listed separately. Elizabeth died in 1875. Her place of burial is unknown. Posey died in 1877, following a violent and bloody shoot-out with the Creek Lighthorse. He is buried in present Tulsa County, Oklahoma. The gravesite is unknown and unmarked.

*ELIZA HULDA POSEY was born in 1849, at Nacogdoches, Texas. She married Joseph M. Allen in 1867. They went to the Indian Territory, receiving an allotment of Creek Indian land. She died in 1930, and is buried in Twin Mounds Cemetery, Tulsa County, Oklahoma.

THE CREEK LAND ALLOTMENTS

Indian Territory had been set aside for the relocation of the Indian tribes to clear the way for white settlement in their former homelands. The treaties were to be binding "as long as the grass grows, and water flows." The lands in Indian Territory occupied by the Five Civilized Tribes were tribally owned. A member of the tribe could locate anywhere in the Nation he wanted. No one had individual title to the land.

The continued clamor by the white settlers wanting land in the West caused the government to create an allotment program for the tribes in Indian Territory. The white citizens convinced the government that a one hundred sixty acre allotment should be plenty for the individual Indian, thereby opening up additional land for others to settle on. The end result was creation of the Dawes Commission, which was ordered to carry out the proclamation. They began taking applications for land allotments after 1896, with final distribution to come after all the citizens of the tribes had been enrolled.

The Posey children, being one-half Creek Indian, qualified as citizens of the Nation. Most came up from Texas to enroll, and receive land. Some sold their land quickly and moved back to Texas. Others kept their allotment and improved it over the years. Some of the Posey and Berryhill descendants were allotted land in present Tulsa County, near Glennpool, and became extremely wealthy when vast pools of oil were discovered there in the early 1900's. Some had land on the fringes that were dry holes and they never shared in the wealth.

The land allotment system created a large number of wealthy politicians and lawyers when the land was divided into individual ownership. Few Indians had experience with land titles, and had no real knowledge of the value of the land that had been allotted to them. Lawyers were appointed by the Commission to oversee their affairs. Many of the Indians were victims of the lawyers and politicians that managed to separate the title from the Indians into their own names--all legally, of course.

Many of the Posey and Berryhill descendants from the early removal still reside along the Arkansas River between Tulsa and Muskogee. Descendants of Benjamin Franklin and Eliza Berryhill still live in Oklahoma, and around Limestone County, Texas. Most of the Posey men were agriculturally oriented, excellent ranchers and horse enthusiasts. Some descendants were ranchers, while some became county agriculture agents. Others followed the rodeo as calf and steer ropers.

THE SONS OF BILL POSEY
AND ELIZABETH WALLACE

The three sons of Bill and Elizabeth Posey: Matthew, Albert Washington and Robert, were sent to live with Bill Posey in the Indian Territory following the death of their mother, Elizabeth, in 1875. Posey was a fugitive, wanted in Texas, with a big reward on his head. The outlaw was killed by the Creek Lighthorse in June, 1877, in events related earlier.

A cousin of Bill Posey's, Lucinda (Hopwood) Smith, took in the Posey sons. Lucinda lived at Concharte Town, southeast of present Tulsa. She had several children of her own, but accepted the Posey sons as members of her own family. Matthew, the oldest, committed some offense, to which Lucinda objected, whereupon she ordered him to leave. Albert Washington and Robert, being sympathetic to their brother, left with him.

The boys were then taken in by a missionary family, the Robertson's, where they resided for a time. Robertson's daughter, Alice Robertson, would be elected to the U.S. Congress in 1920. She was the first, and only woman, elected to the U.S. Congress from Oklahoma, and only the second woman elected from the United States at the time.

All the boys went to Idaho, about 1890, to work as ranch hands. Albert Washington worked as a bronc buster on a ranch for several years. Matthew and Robert worked as cowboys. Albert had worked and put together a small horse herd of his own, but the herd was stolen by his brothers, who headed back for Indian Territory after selling the horses. Albert Washington had a forgiving nature and never held a grudge over the incident, it was said.

Learning of the land allotments in Indian Territory, they all returned and made application for their one hundred sixty acres. Each received an allotment. Eventually the homestead allotments were sold and Matthew and Albert Washington returned to the West, where they would remain except for occasional visits with relatives.

*MATTHEW ANDREW POSEY, was born September 11, 1866, at Waco, McLennan County, Texas. He was named for Elizabeth's brother, Matthew Wallace. The Andrew name came from his father. He was one-quarter Creek Indian. He lost an arm in the early 1890's, according to family sources, while running with the Dalton outlaw gang in the Territory. The shoulder was blown away by a shotgun blast. Matthew was able to overcome the handicap and accomplish many tasks, including rolling a Bull Durham cigarette, one-handed.

He married Rebecca Hannah, at Wagoner, Oklahoma, in 1907. Shortly after the marriage they went to Idaho. Three children were born to the marriage: Inez, born in 1911, in Idaho; Lysle, born 1913, in Idaho, and Geniveve, born in 1918, in Oklahoma. Matthew Andrew died in 1950, at age eighty four. He is buried at Phoenix, Arizona, where the family lived in later years.

*ALBERT WASHINGTON POSEY was born February 7, 1869, at Waco, McLennan County, Texas. He was one-quarter Creek Indian, and received a land allotment in the Creek Nation. His Washington name came from Elizabeth's father, Washington S. Wallace. It is not known where the Albert name originated, but perhaps from Albert Aikman. He married Mary Ann Dayley, December 8, 1893, at Basin , Idaho. Ten children were born to the marriage: Wallace Leroy, 1895; Leonard Earl, 1896; Elsie Myrtle, 1898; Elmer Carl, 1900; Nina Elvira, 1904; Ora Elizabeth, 1907; Albert Melvin and Delbert Kelvin, twins, 1909; Arkie Ann, 1917 and T.C. Posey, 1920. Albert Washington died June 7, 1953, at age eighty four. Mary Ann died April 8, 1955. Both are buried at Basin, Idaho.

*ROBERT A. POSEY was born June 21, 1871, at Waco, McLennan County, Texas. He was one-quarter Creek Indian, and received a land allotment in the Creek Nation. He was married to Flora E. Hardy, of Utah, in 1890, at Basin, Idaho. They had three children: Lee A., born 1893, in Idaho; Mary E., born 1895, at Red Fork, Indian Territory, and William A. Posey, born in 1897, in Idaho. Robert died of a stomach disorder in February, 1901, at age thirty. He is buried at Red Fork, Indian Territory, now a part of West Tulsa.

*HENRY A. POSEY was born in 1877, near Concharte Town, I.T., to William Andrew Jackson Posey and Susan (Riggs) Posey. He was one-fourth Creek Indian and received a land allotment in the Creek Nation. After his father was killed he lived with his mother near Tulsa, and later moved to near Holdenville. He married a woman named Mary, and they had one child. Maiden name of the wife, and the name of the child is not known. They lived at Wagoner, I.T. Henry died June 10, 1904. His burial place is unknown, but believed to be at Wagoner. Susan may have married again to a man named Grayson, for Henry was enumerated in an 1895 Creek census as Henry Grayson. He claimed his birth name of Posey for the Creek land allotments, however.

CYNTHIA ANN PARKER AND THE COMANCHES

Nothing was heard from the Parker or Plummer captives for more than six years following the 1836 massacre at Fort Parker, in Limestone County. Then, young James Plummer was brought into Fort Gibson, Indian Territory, where he was ransomed to the army. Soon after, a band of white buffalo hunters came upon a Comanche village and found his mother, Rachael Plummer, working for her captors. They negotiated her release. Young Plummer and his mother were returned to family and friends in Anderson County, but Rachel's health, and spirit, was broken and she soon died.

There had been no sightings or word concerning the young Cynthia Ann and John Parker. But unknown to their white relatives and friends, Cynthia Ann and John were growing up as Comanches. Cynthia Ann became the wife of the Comanche Chief, Peta Nocona, at age fifteen. Nocona was the proud and robust warrior of the Naconi Clan. Cynthia Ann was speaking fluent Comanche. Young John was growing up to be a daring Comanche warrior. He often led his own raids on Mexican ranches in horse-stealing forays. Both Parker's were Comanche in every respect.

Cynthia Ann soon bore Chief Nocona a strong, healthy son. He was destined to be one of the Southwest's most daring and skillful tribal leaders. He was given the last name of his mother, which was highly unusual, but he became known as Quanah Parker. For twenty four years, Cynthia Ann had lived like a Comanche. She had been only six years old when taken captive at Fort Parker. She remembered little about her life among the whites. She and young John roamed the Llano Estacado of Western Texas and the Indian Territory with the tribe.

On a cold, bleak morning of December 18, 1860, Captain Sul Ross and a group of Texas Rangers discovered a Comanche hunting camp. Moving cautiously down a draw, the group surprised the sleeping camp, killing most of the braves. Ross noticed a fleeing woman on horseback with a papoose rack strapped onto the saddle. They overtook the woman and baby, and noticed she appeared to be a white woman with blue eyes. Through a Mexican interpretor who spoke Comanche, they learned she was Cynthia Ann Parker. She spoke no English, but recognized her Christian name. The baby was a girl child, named "Prairie Flower." Neither Chief Nokona or Quanah Parker were in camp when the Rangers attacked.

Cynthia Ann, and the baby, were returned to her white relatives, who now lived in Anderson County. She did not belong in the civilized culture any longer. She was a complete stranger to her relatives, and could not even communicate with them. She sat for long periods of time staring into the west--longing for her husband, Nocona, and her son Quanah. She grieved herself into a melancholy state, refusing to eat. Prairie Flower soon died, perhaps from the abrupt change of diet. Four years after being returned to her white relatives, Cynthia Ann died. Many said the death was a result of a broken heart. She was buried in Fosterville Cemetery, near Poyner, Texas, in the spring of 1864.

Quanah Parker succeeded his father as chief, and his Comanches would rule the plains for another ten years. The Texas settlers were still subject to vicious raids. The Comanches were the finest horsemen among all the Indian tribes. Their mobility allowed them to strike swiftly and mightily, and be gone before retaliatory measures could be organized by their white enemy. The Comanches were called "Lords of the Plains," and for good reason. But the white settlers were gaining in numbers, and the Texas Rangers were beginning to become more effective with superior firepower. The Comanche was being pushed farther back into West Texas, and to their villages in Indian Territory.

The undoing of the Comanche was at Adobe Walls, in the Texas panhandle. Word had reached Quanah that white people were there, and it would be an easy mark. Adobe Walls was nothing more than an old buffalo hunter's camp, constructed of sun-baked adobe bricks. It was abandoned more than it was occupied. The Comanche warriors arrived at the camp at sun-up, and prepared to lay siege to the occupants. They did not know that the buffalo hunters were now equipped with the new repeating rifles. Their aim was deadly, and the warriors were cut to ribbons. For three days the siege continued, with Chief Quanah counting more and more of his best warrior's dead. Then the soldiers began to tighten the noose, arriving from Camp Supply and Fort Sill, in the Territory, and from Fort Gordon, in Texas, and Fort Union, in New Mexico.

Quanah Parker then gathered the last remaining members of his cherished Antelope Band and started the long trek to Fort Sill. There they would surrender and be placed onto the nearby reservation. On the twenty second day of June, 1875, the Lords of the Plains rode quietly, but proudly into the parade area of Fort Sill and peacefully surrendered to the Army.

Settling on a ranch Near Cache, Oklahoma, Quanah Parker became an outstanding citizen and influential leader of several tribes. He was appointed judge of the court concerning Indian affairs for the Wichita, Caddo, Comanche, Kiowa and Apache reservations in Oklahoma. He had six wives and eighteen children.

In 1910, the government granted him permission to have the remains of his beloved mother, Cynthia Ann Parker, moved to the Indian Burial Ground behind the historic Post Oak Mission at Cache, Oklahoma. In 1911, Quanah Parker died and was laid to rest beside his mother, who, as a small child was kidnapped and raised by the Comanche. Thus ended the last of the Indian Wars on the plains. In 1956, both historic figures were re-interred, with full military honors, at Fort Sill Memorial Cemetery.

The white Parker descendants in Texas and the Indian Parker descendants in Oklahoma have annual family reunions.

This may be proof that time does heal wounds.

ABOUT THE AUTHOR

    More than forty years as a newspaper man qualifies Bill Lehmann to be a professional observer of people. He has lived life joyously surrounding himself with people, the great and the humble, the politically powerful, and the disenfranchised, the affluent and the impoverished, alcoholics, teetotalers, historians, artists, drifters, oil drillers, poets, preachers, and musicians. His life is richer for having known all those he writes about.

    As newspaper editor in several Oklahoma towns and as publisher and General Manager of the *Guthrie Daily Leader*, Lehmann used his "tons of newsprint and barrels of ink" to advance issues, both grand and meek, to touch and improve the quality of life in his communities—Laredo, Ponca City, Pawhuska, and Guthrie.

    Lehmann has always been interested in genealogy. This book is a result of years of research all across Texas in his quest to find out the truth about his ancestors.

    The award-winning newspaperman never ceased observing people, enjoying life, and pondering the past and the future…sometimes in the company of another old friend, Jack Daniels. He died in 2016.

    Lehmann is the author of two others books, *An Okie from Muskogee Recalls Growing Up in the Dirty '30s* and *After the Parade,* both available on amazon.com.

Made in the USA
Middletown, DE
03 June 2023

32017543R00116